Daily Bread,
Holy Meal

Opening the Gifts of Holy Communion

Samuel Torvend

Augsburg Fortress

DAILY BREAD, HOLY MEAL
Opening the Gifts of Holy Communion

Copyright © 2004 Augsburg Fortress. All rights reserved. Except for brief quotations in critical articles or reviews, no part of this book may be reproduced without prior written permission from the publisher. Write to: Permissions, Augsburg Fortress, Publishers, P. O. Box 1209, Minneapolis, MN 55440-1209.

Unless otherwise indicated, Scripture quotations are from the New Revised Standard Version Bible © 1989 Division of Christian Education of the National Council of the Churches of Christ in the United States of America. Used by permission.

Editors: Suzanne Burke, Robert Farlee, Jessica Hillstrom
Cover and interior design: Laurie Ingram
Cover photo © Richard Cummins/CORBIS

ISBN 0-8066-5106-7

Manufactured in the U.S.A.

07   06   05   04   1   2   3   4   5   6   7   8   9   10

For Silas and Alice Kjesbu Torvend who fed me the bread of life

at home and brought me to the Lord's table,

for the hospitality of Rebecca and Frank Rainsberger,

for table fellowship with Stephen Crippen and Andrew Stone,

for the word and melody of Susan and David Cherwien,

for the people of Trinity Lutheran Church Parkland who listened to

the ideas and said, Say more,

I offer thanks.

Contents

Introduction

In the bread, there is life

In 1902, Prudence Van Buskirk and her husband, Andrew Jackson Mills, departed Cowen, West Virginia, never to return. They left behind the impoverished mining communities of the region, a place that would soon witness bloody clashes between the National Guard and miners attempting to organize into labor unions. They were lured to the Pacific Northwest by posters and word-of-mouth that promised cheap land, wild forests, and rivers filled with salmon. Along with countless Americans and newly arrived immigrant families, they were part of that great flow toward the western reaches of the continent where they created one of the most prosperous fishing and agricultural centers in the nation. "Come west to the Garden of Eden," read one advertisement, "there is bread enough for everyone."

Ollie Mae Mills was eight months old when she was bundled into a train with her parents and left the Appalachian Mountains for the western slopes of Washington's Cascade Range. Growing up in the foothills of Mount Rainier, close to the Cowlitz River and Winston Creek, she and her family had little in wealth but were rich in the natural bounty of the river, the forest, and the land. Working as fisher folk, tree-toppers, and farmers, they were able to create a modest Eden where there was bread enough for everyone. Indeed, as she grew up, Ollie Mills became a competent baker of drop rolls, shortbread, and corn muffins—the simple breads found in farming communities throughout the region. But her specialty was golden molasses bread—a dense, moist, fragrant brown bread studded with golden raisins soaked in a bit of brandy—made from a recipe that accompanied her family on its long journey from the mean poverty of the eastern mountains to the natural abundance of the western valleys.

In 1921, she married Niel Kjesbu, a young Norwegian American who had emigrated from Starbuck, Minnesota. A teacher by training, Niel was also a gifted musician who, at one time, had hoped to become a Lutheran pastor. Together, they had four children, each one surrounded by music and the fragrance of baking molasses bread. But they also had this: the experience of welcoming friends and strangers to the family table where their mother's golden bread was served, broken, and shared. And, in time, each child possessed the recipe itself, making possible the multiplication of this one dense and delicious loaf in numerous households of children and grandchildren.

As the children of Alice Kjesbu and Silas Torvend, my sister, Rebecca, and I now have this recipe, written in our mother's hand, an inheritance from our maternal great grandmother, Prudence, and our grandmother, Ollie Mae. This bread, baked by our mother for birthday breakfasts and holidays, now is a living gift to pass on to friends and family, to future generations who live in this evergreen Eden and anywhere else people need bread. But we have more than a recipe; we possess the many meanings and associations that surround this particular kind of bread. As we smell and then savor its taste, we certainly enjoy delicious bread. The very things drawn from this earth—wheat, molasses, brandy, raisins, and yeast—nourish life, and because they nourish life, they gladden the heart. *In hoc pane est vita,* the medieval proverb proclaimed: "In this bread, there is life." Yet one also tastes the labor of those who spread the seed and harvested the wheat; those who refined cane sugar into the dark syrup of molasses; those who planted, tended, and harvested the grape vine. One not only bites into dense bread, but into the very things of this earth that make the bread possible.

Taste the bread and you taste the memory of impoverishment and early death among the coal miners and the struggle to be free from a life of indebted servitude to the owners of the mines. The bread also holds the memory of the arduous journey to a land filled to over-flowing with salmon, apples, and deep red onions. Because this bread expresses the memory of the family, it evokes a common history from England, Norway, West Virginia, Minnesota, and Washington. It allows us to tell the stories of our beloved dead and the newly born so that the past and the future become present in the moment as we break, share, and eat it. And this, too: the loaf is too large for one and must be shared with the many; it cannot be hoarded or eaten alone. It is not "my" but "our" bread. Yet it is not simply "our" bread that only "we" eat: the gift of this bread asks to be shared with friends, in-laws, visitors, and strangers. Thus, in the history of this bread, people from diverse economic, educational, ethnic, and social backgrounds have shared dense morsels of the golden loaf. Baptists, Buddhists, Catholics, Episcopalians, Jews, Lutherans, Quakers, and people with no religion whatsoever have enjoyed every bite.

"Give us this day our daily bread," says the prayer of Christians. But that word *bread* always means more than just one thing. My grandmother used molasses because it was the only sweetener poor people could afford until sugar prices plummeted during the 1930s. Today, even though sugar is fairly inexpensive, we wouldn't dream of substituting the syrup with sugar granules. So, for us, it is also the bread of poor people and a living reminder of the poor who surround the well-educated, middle-class grandchildren of Ollie and Niel Kjesbu, Emma and Benjamin Torvend. It is the bread shared at family gatherings, the staple food that has marked births, birthdays, anniversaries, holidays, and deaths. Yes, bread may hold life, but it holds memory as well. Indeed, my sister's toddler son will receive the recipe at the right moment, the list of ingredients and the making of the bread linking the generations from the nineteenth to the twenty-first centuries. Will he ever use it? Who knows? But it is his legacy, this ordinary bread transfigured by memory and hope.

There is always more

It should come as no surprise that bread is one of the central images of the Bible; a simple and daily food, yet one charged with a variety of meanings: the unleavened bread of Passover, the manna in the wilderness, the showbread of the Temple, the barley loaves Jesus blesses and shares with a crowd—bread as rescue from oppression, as sustenance on a perilous journey, as sacrifice offered to God, as peasant bread shared with hungry people. Today, when theologians and other scholars point to the many meanings of bread in the Bible or in the history of Christianity, they use the term *symbol*. Although conventional wisdom might suggest that *symbol* refers to something empty of meaning, as in "it's only symbolic," the wisdom of the Christian tradition, steeped in reflection on the Bible, recognizes that its collection of images and practices, persons and events always, always holds more than one meaning. To say that breaking and sharing bread is a "symbolic activity" is to claim, simply but profoundly, that breaking bread possesses more than one meaning for a family, a community, or a culture.

It's clear, for instance, that eating bread sustains physical life, but we also know from our own experience, it involves much more. It is also a gift from the natural world and a sign of human ingenuity and labor. Bread is shared to express friendship and, at times, withheld by those who are at odds with each other. "I will not break bread with him" is not only an expression of the reluctance to break a piece of bread and pass it to someone else; it is a terrible sign of a relationship gone awry. Choice in bread not only represents taste, it also symbolizes social and economic status. Most poor Americans can't afford the "artisan" breads that fill the higher-end markets. Consequently the poor must buy the less expensive white bread that holds little nutritional value. Bread is not a "neutral" thing; it is "symbolic" of other realities. There is, indeed, more to bread than meets the eye.

In the same vein, it is not uncommon for Christians, who are a bread-eating people, to speak metaphorically of Jesus as the bread of life, sweet manna from heaven, or the gift of finest wheat, yet none of these images or meanings exhausts the richness and depth of the biblical witness nor the experience of Christians in their encounter with this One who holds the many together. One image, one meaning will simply not do. Indeed, the desire to reduce the figure of Jesus of Nazareth or the bread of life to only one meaning or small truth is simply an unfortunate sign of a circumscribed imagination that fails to recognize rich meanings in that great treasure of the Bible and the experience of Christians. There is always a greater depth; there is always more. This realization should not be surprising given that the New Testament itself holds at least four distinctive portraits of Jesus and the disciples in the four gospels. Clearly, the early Christians who established the list of books that constitute the New Testament welcomed a measure of diversity as they attempted to communicate the significance of Jesus of Nazareth for diverse and different communities.

No wonder, then, that when Christians speak of eating bread and drinking from a cup of wine, they use not one but a variety of images: the breaking of the bread, Eucharist, the Lord's supper, Holy Communion, Mass. One image, for instance, interprets this action as grateful reception of God's gifts of food and drink, what some early Christians called "the breaking of the bread" (Acts 2:42; Luke 24:30-31). Another image views eating bread and drinking from the cup as the occasion for thanksgiving to God (Mark 14:23), while another one focuses on the One who keeps many meals and this particular meal of the Lord's supper with the church on the Lord's day (1 Cor. 11:23-26). A fourth image highlights the communal dimension of this action in which those who eat and drink are bound into a "holy communion" with each other (1 Cor. 10:16-17). At the same time, it emphasizes the gift of reconciliation or forgiveness that rests at the heart of Jesus' words in the Gospel of Matthew (26:27-28). Yet this emphasis on the communion of the community is set next to another image that emphasizes the dismissal (*missa,* mass) from the communion into the "city," the larger community, there to announce good news (Luke 24:33-35).

One image emphasizes the simple human action of breaking bread set next to the act of giving thanks to God. Another image highlights the Risen One as the host of this supper set next to a community that keeps this meal publicly so that anyone may witness it. One more image invites those who eat the bread to recognize that such eating unites them with all who eat from the one loaf. Yet this, too, is set next to the impulse that moves those who have shared the meal to enter a world marked by much beauty and untold suffering, great wealth and countless hungry people. Thus, the biblical metaphors that point to some of the many meanings of this central Christian practice can be set next to each other—juxtaposed as it were—to highlight the lively tensions that abound in receiving this daily bread and keeping this holy communion. Eating bread is set next to God the giver of all good things. Recognizing the risen Christ is set next to the communal dimension of the supper where there is forgiveness. Communion in these good things that binds the gathering together is set next to the dispersal that dismisses the people into a world of great need.

The relatively stable middle-class grandchildren of poor people from Appalachia and immigrants from Minnesota could choose to forget the struggle to survive that actually made their lives possible.

But the golden bread, made with poor people's sweetener, calls us to recognize that poverty and hunger are on the increase across our land. In like manner, those who gather to receive "the gifts of God for the people of God" are called to remember that the One they name "sweet manna" and "bread of life" shared barley loaves, peasant bread, as a poor person with the oppressed of Roman Palestine as a sign that "God is filling the hungry with good things" (Luke 1:53). Lord's supper and daily bread, thanksgiving and forgiveness, communal gathering and service among the hungry: not one without the other. Such are the gifts of this holy and uncommon communion.

1
Let the Vineyards Be Fruitful

The gift of broad fields

Although the population of North America in 1865 was largely settled in rural areas and small towns throughout the eastern seaboard and the central region of the continent, the past 150 years have witnessed a remarkable shift in population concentration to urban and suburban areas. For instance, more than 75 percent of the U.S. population now lives in large, sprawling cities. The people who labor in most universities, medical research centers, national and international businesses, museums and concert halls, media and transportation hubs, church headquarters, and governmental offices live in these urban centers and are shaped in their imaginations, consciously or unconsciously, by the joys and stress, miseries and advantages of urban living. Of course, if one has grown up in the mega-cities that straddle the coasts or dot the central plains, all this seems simply natural.

During that movement of the nineteenth century to urban locations that coincided with the emergence of manufacturing centers, railroad expansion, and new waves of immigration, our collective connection to the rhythms and work of rural, agricultural life slowly unraveled. This is not to say that farms have been abandoned or that contemporary North Americans don't idealize rural life or the relatively uninhabited regions of the country. After all, who hasn't longed to rest by a wilderness lake or telecommute from a quiet farmhouse when caught in the middle of unmoving traffic and the seemingly frantic schedules that, alas, seem to be part and parcel of urban life? Most polls seem to suggest, however, that urban North Americans are not yet prepared to return to a rhythm of living shaped by the rising and setting of the sun, seasonal fluctuations, and the intensive labor of producing a crop or caring for a herd. Most North Americans fly over waves of grain and drive quickly by holding pens filled with snorting pigs and clucking chickens, glad for the ham in the freezer, chicken strips in the microwave, and loaves of presliced bread in the kitchen.

Perhaps this is why it is not surprising to hear children and college students suggest with utter sincerity that food comes from grocery stores or markets. Perhaps this is why one rarely hears prayers for farmers and fields in urban and suburban churches. And perhaps this is why such notable writers as Annie Dillard (*Pilgrim at Tinker Creek*) and Kathleen Norris (*Dakota*), narrators of life by a rural creek and in a Midwest farm community, have met with such remarkable success as if they were reporters from a foreign country, keen observers of exotic lands and long-forgotten people one normally glimpses in the *National Geographic*. Our historical, physical, and imaginative distance from field and farm—from the natural grace of soil and seed—can make it difficult for much of the population to grasp the simple declaration of Jesus that summarizes the mystery of death and life: "Unless a grain of wheat falls into the earth and dies, it remains just a single grain; but if it dies, it bears much fruit" (John 12:24). Without field and grain, there is no stalk, no separation from chaff, no grinding, no flour, and no bread. Without field and shoot, there is no vine, no grape, no crushing and separation, no ferment, no wine. No wonder so many urban Christians in North America don't balk when

round, thin wafers that have the consistency of fish food are present-
ed to them as bread or when grape juice is offered as wine. As the
owner of an Italian delicatessen said to me recently, "The younger
generations are so used to processed foods and artificial drinks that
they think these are 'real' things and back away from the pungent
smell of cheese or a dark wine filled with the bittersweet smell of
berries."

Yet many Christians sing these words every Sunday as bread and
wine are placed on a table of stone or wood: "Let the vineyards be
fruitful, Lord, and fill to the brim our cup of blessing. Gather a harvest from the seeds that were sown that we may be fed with the bread
of life" (*Lutheran Book of Worship*, p. 66). Still others sing: "I would
feed you with the finest of wheat, and with honey from the rock I
would satisfy you" (Ps. 81:16). At the heart of the Christian liturgy,
then, is this potent word that points the worshiping assembly to the
broad fields, out there beyond the city limits, where the grain died in
order to become this bread that sustains human life, where the grape
was crushed in order to produce the wine poured into this cup. In an
urban culture at some distance from wheat fields and vineyards, these
words—"seeds were sown"—sneak into the consciousness of the
assembly, to rest dormant throughout a lifetime or spring to awareness when experience of the field connects with the experience of
food and drink. So my suburban students and I go on a Saturday to
Mother Earth Farm in the lush Puyallup Valley where we join other
volunteers in planting seeds and bulbs that will one day burst forth as
food for the hungry and homeless of our region. Most of us have no
idea of the ever-present care and risk involved in planting, tending,
defending, and reaping a harvest subject to the ravages of insects, animals, thieves, and weather. Yet the experience of the field, its labor,
and risk force us to hear anew the words we sing on Sunday: Let the
vineyards be fruitful . . . gather a harvest from the seeds that were
sown. Here, here in the soil, with hands dirty and neck sunburned,

praying like any medieval peasant for "favorable weather," here is where the seed and the vine flourish or fail. Here is the source of food. In the fields there is life.

The greening power of God

The odd thing is that when Christians forget the fields and vineyards, when they begin to focus solely on themselves apart from the creation (what theologians call an "anthropocentric" or human-focused view), they begin to forget many of the significant biblical and theological claims that form the collective wisdom of Christians regarding the natural world: for instance, that the creation is a growing, diverse, and tangible sign of the Creator's desire to sustain the very life the Creator continues to bring into existence. An ancient hymn to the goodness of God's creating and tending invites the reader or singer to consider the natural world from the larger perspective, from a "cosmic" viewpoint:

> You set the earth on its foundations, so that it shall never be shaken.
> You cover it with the deep as with a garment . . .
> You make springs gush forth in the valleys;
> they flow between the hills, giving drink to every wild animal . . .
>
> You cause the grass to grow for the cattle, and plants for people to use,
> to bring forth food from the earth, and wine to gladden the human heart,
> oil to make the face shine, and bread to strengthen the human heart . . .
>
> O LORD, how manifold are your works!
> In wisdom you have made them all; the earth is full of your creatures . . .

These all look to you to give them their food in due season;
when you give to them, they gather it up;
when you open your hand, they are filled with good things.
(Ps. 104: 5, 6, 10-11, 14-15, 24, 27-28)

In the eleventh century, the German Benedictine nun Hildegard of Bingen, a biblical scholar, gardener, musician, preacher, and herbalist, wrote in her many poems that the "wisdom that made all creatures" was nothing less than the greening power of God's creating word. The word of God, she wrote, is a power, a vital power charged with greenness. So enraptured was Hildegard of this natural grace alive in the earth and its many diverse creations, that she coined her own word— *viriditas* or "verdant greening"—to name this power that overcomes bareness in the earth and in human life. No wonder she would speak of Christ as the "green figure" whose mission is to bring *viriditas* to humans who are "withered" or "dried up" by the presence of an enervating, wasting wind that can parch the creation. Where there is the presence of God, there is the verdant life that one can see in the garden, orchard, or field.

Clearly Hildegard was writing from the perspective of someone who has knowledge of the earth and the field and thus her daily experience allowed her to focus on the many agricultural metaphors and stories that fill the Bible. Indeed, she suggests that when this greening word of God takes human form, Mary's womb brings forth wheat from which a great feast is prepared for all humanity. Perhaps this is a word play on the meaning of the word *Bethlehem* ("house of bread") or simply a reflection of the medieval agricultural imagination that enjoyed the natural symbols so prominent in John's gospel: water (7:37), light (8:12), bread (6:35), or vine (15:1). To modern ears that may be used to hearing of Christ as a merciful lord, beautiful savior, or friend of sinners (all images derived from human relationships), these nature images may at first sound odd: God as greening power and Christ as wheat? But I'd argue that in their oddity and very earthiness, they simply underscore a fundamental claim alive in most Christian communities: God is present to and working through all things, not just the individual's spirit or ego but also human bodies and the body of this earth.

Less than four hundred years after Hildegard, Luther found himself locked in a debate over the meaning of the sentence in the creed that states, "He ascended into heaven and is seated at the right hand of the Father." Luther's Protestant opponents argued that if Christ is seated at the right hand of God he couldn't be palpably present in the bread and wine of the Lord's supper. Echoing a sentiment alive among many contemporary North American Christians, these opponents taught that the supper was necessary in order to remember Christ's last supper and be reminded of God's promise of forgiveness, but Christ could not be present in two places at once: in heaven and to the Christian assembly in or with the natural elements of bread and wine. Against this claim Luther offered, in frustration, his response: only a numbskull who doesn't know the scriptures would think that God has a "right hand." The "hand of God," Luther argued, is a metaphorical reference to God's power and presence throughout the universe, the earth, and the creation. Thus, Christ did not ascend to a distant heavenly throne to be crowned prince of the world. Rather, he was raised into the power and presence of God for whom there is no limitation of time and place. He has become, to quote Paul, "a life-giving Spirit."

Christ is everywhere because the "right hand" of God is everywhere. Wherever God is offering life, there is Christ, "free and unbounded." Just as one's personality, the animating center of a human being, is revealed through the unique body and capacities of the person, so Christ, the vivifying center of the cosmos "through whom all things came into being" (John 1:3), is revealed through God's gracious gift of the natural world. By making this claim, Luther was not suggesting that if one eats an apple or plucks a flower that one is eating or plucking Christ. For heaven's sakes, the man was not a literalist. Rather, he was suggesting with John that Christ, the creating Word of God, is powerfully present everywhere, offering life and health through, to, and for the creation, a veritable energy field "creating, effecting, and preserving all things."

What, then, do we find in the Hebrew psalmist, the gardening nun, and the German reformer? Perhaps it is the insistence that God's movement is always a movement or an advance *toward* the creation, toward humanity, with nothing less than the promise of life. I walk across the astonishingly beautiful university campus where I teach—surrounded by towering fir trees, verdant lawns, brightly colored rhododendrons, and splendid oak trees—and think how lovely it all is, as if I work in a park. I think the psalmist, the nun, and the reformer would point to all this greening power, to all the wide wheat fields and thriving vineyards of the land, as nothing less than the verdant offer of life and health, an offer made without discrimination. Thus the Christian assembly can sing at table a song of praise that pulls one far beyond the little "me" into the greening power alive in the cosmos:

> Holy God, Holy One, Holy Three!
> You beyond the galaxies,
> you under the oceans,
> you inside the leaves,
> you pouring down rain,
> you opening the flower,
> you feeding the insects,
> you giving us your image.
> (RW6, p. 64)

Wise stewards of the earth

The other thing that happens when Christians forget the fields and vineyards is they desert their baptismal and eucharistic mandate to serve as public stewards of land, air, and water. At first that might sound odd: baptismal identity and public stewardship of land? Aren't government agencies or environmental watchdog groups supposed to care for the land, the air, and the water? Well, that would be the easy way to answer the question. But, again, I don't think the biblical and theological wisdom of the Christian community lets one off the hook that easily.

Consider that a person is baptized in water. It is hard to imagine that any community would allow a child or an adult to be baptized in polluted water or a basin filled with toxic chemicals. Although no hard-and-fast rule governs what water is used in baptism, it goes without saying that most if not all Christian communities intend to use fresh and clean water when they celebrate baptism. But here's the great irony. Where I live, we are grateful for the rain, the snow, the many creeks and rivers, lakes, and deep bays that surround us, yet no one wants to wash their baptismal candidates in the waters of the local bay or the river that empties into it; they are both sites viewed by the government as degraded and polluted and in immediate need of cleaning, waterways so polluted by manufacturers that it will take years before any life emerges from the muck. Drink from it? Are you kidding? Yet the psalm praises God as the one who makes "springs gush forth in the valleys . . . giving drink to every wild animal" (Ps. 104:10, 11). Is there not an incongruity, here, between the Creator's living gift of fresh, clean water and the pollution of these waters over the last 150 years?

As a child, I was taught many stories from the Hebrew Bible. In sermons, songs, school lessons, and summer camps we learned what our teachers called the ancestors of Christians, beginning with Adam and Eve and progressing through Noah, Abraham and Sarah, Isaac, Jacob, Joseph, Moses and Miriam, David and Solomon. I know that we read both creation stories in the Book of Genesis (1:1—2:3; 2:4—3:24), but if memory serves me well, we spent little time discussing the creation or the natural world itself. Rather we focused on people (the anthropocentric view) rather than the creation or human beings as members of a larger and diverse creation (the cosmocentric view). Did our schooling simply reflect the view of the American Enlightenment, espoused by Thomas Jefferson and other Deists, that God created the world, set it in motion, and then handed it over to human beings to master it for their own purposes? Indeed, I can't remember that we ever spent a second studying the profound claim that God owns the land that human beings "rent," as it were, during their tenure in this world. "The land is mine," says the LORD, "with me you are but aliens and tenants" (Lev. 25:23). Some scholars might claim that the Hebrew reference to land only refers to the Promised Land, but I want to expand the claim. I think the anonymous psalmist, Hildegard, and Luther invite us to think about the whole creation— water, animals, fields, humans, air, trees, fish, vineyards—as God's diverse, growing, yet fragile domain, as gift and blessing that nourish life. The psalm, the poetry, and reformation argument wisely critique the separation of God from creation and creation from human creatures; they express a deep wisdom in both Judaism and Christianity that sees God, creation, and humanity intimately linked together, as an organic whole.

Do Christians hold any responsibility for the streams, air, and fields that constitute human habitation? Well, probably not, if one imagines that God's purpose, in the end, is to rescue souls from the entrapment of the body and the prison of earthly life, to whisk them away at last to a dematerialized existence in a bodiless heaven. That is, after all, one model that has wielded enormous influence in the Christian tradition. The problem with this view, however, is that it has some difficulty coming to terms with the Christian confession that God creates a good creation filled with diverse and interdependent creatures, and that God becomes embodied in the incarnation and promises the resurrection of the body, not the immortality of the soul. If life with God is a communion of Spirit to spirit or Soul to soul, then one doesn't really need a body—the human body or earth's body. One only needs patience until one's departure from this "vale of tears" or, to use the polite language of the media, until we "pass."

But this is not the only model. Another view, what some scholars call the "ecological" model in the biblical and theological tradition, affirms this earth as the living gift to which God invites human stewardship and care until "the creation itself will be set free from its bondage to decay and will obtain the freedom of the glory of the children of God" (Rom. 8:21). The apocalyptic imagination, so vibrant in contemporary western consciousness and narrated visually in film after film, dwells on the end of the earth as one great cataclysmic conflagration in which everything but a few "saved" souls is burned to a crisp. In contrast, the ecological imagination claims its God-given responsibility for this earth now and looks forward to that time when God will not destroy all things but renew them, *here on earth*. Not surprisingly, the very people who sing, "Let the vineyards be fruitful, Lord," also sing, "and give us a foretaste of the feast to come." Feast, not fire and brimstone.

I sometimes wonder, then, whether Christians think about the implications of the words they speak together as bread and wine are placed on the altar: "We dedicate our lives to the care and redemption of all that you have made." Really? Listen again: "We dedicate our lives to the care and redemption of all that you have made." Doesn't this promise commit the Christian assembly to serve as public stewards of the creation that, from the perspective of faith, is gift and blessing from God? The assembly may readily confess at table, "The universe declares your praise: beyond the stars, beneath the sea, within each cell, with every breath" (RW6, p. 68). Yet the alarming evidence of increasing human waste of the earth should keep one mindful that seas, fields, and the air itself can be turned from blessing to curse. It is not uncommon for Christians to confess that they meet the Risen One in the breaking of the bread. But do they not also meet, in the words of that beloved hymn, the "king of creation"? And if they meet the One through whom "all things came into being" (John 1:3), do they not also meet the creation, beloved by God and created through the power of God's greening word? It may well be the assembly's "duty and joy to give thanks and praise to God" at the breaking of the bread. Is it not also one's duty and joy to care for the very things God loves?

> "Give us today our daily bread." Here we consider the poor breadbasket—the needs of our body and our life on earth. It is a brief and simple word, but very comprehensive. When you say and ask for "daily bread," you ask for everything that is necessary in order to have and enjoy daily bread and, on the contrary, against everything that interferes with enjoying it. You must therefore expand and extend your thoughts to include not just the oven or the flour bin, but also the broad fields and the whole land that produce and provide our daily bread and all kinds of sustenance for us. For if God did not cause grain to grow and did not bless it and preserve it in the field, we could never have a loaf of bread to take from the oven or to set upon the table (The Large Catechism, *The Book of Concord*, pp. 449–450).

What more need one say but "thank you" in word and deed?

For reflection and discussion

1. In your reflection on this chapter, what did you find congruent or incongruent with your understanding of the natural world?
2. Describe, if you can, an experience of the land that provoked wonder, thanksgiving, or concern within you.
3. The Christian community uses water, bread, wine, and sometimes olive oil in its sacramental celebrations. Many church houses are built

of natural materials (e.g., wood, stone) from the region. Hymns and songs sung in worship praise God as creator of all these gifts. What actions or texts in the liturgy have helped you recognize that "heaven and earth are full of the glory of God"?

4. The Christian tradition has supported both domination and care of the natural world. How do the insights of the psalmist, Hildegard, and Luther confirm or contradict your understanding of the natural world from a Christian perspective?

5. Reflect for a moment on the words offered by the worshiping assembly that commit the assembly to the "care and redemption of all that you [God] have made." How is Christian service to the natural world embodied in your congregation?

2
To Give Our Thanks and Praise

Every common bush aflame with God

Teach a college course on Christian theology and inevitably you have to deal with that significant word, *revelation*. The word itself is not all that difficult to understand. It simply refers to the act of disclosing or revealing something to a human being. For instance, "I love you very much; will you marry me?" is a deeply revelatory statement and question filled with the possibility of creating a new reality for the one who speaks and the one who hears and responds. At the same time, revelation occurs without words. When a mother patiently feeds her toddler son, she engages in a deeply revelatory action, one that expresses her desire to share food, satisfy his hunger, ensure his health, promote his life, and contribute to his happiness. Through both words and actions, humans disclose or reveal their intentions to each other.

When Christian theologians use the term *revelation*, they are usually referring to the manner in which God communicates with and discloses God's intentions for the creation. "Earth's crammed with heaven and every common bush aflame with God," wrote Elizabeth Barrett Browning, "but only those who see take off their shoes; the

rest stand round picking blackberries." Not unlike Hildegard of
Bingen who saw the whole earth charged with *viriditas*, God's greening presence, Browning suggests that the earth itself is a revelation or
disclosure from God. Perhaps the psalmist would concur:

> The heavens are telling the glory of God; and the firmament
>   proclaims God's handiwork.
> Day to day pours forth speech, and night to night declares
>   knowledge.
> There is no speech, nor are there words; their voice is not heard;
> yet their voice goes out through all the earth, and their words to
>   the end of the world.
> (Ps. 19:1-4)

There is room in the Christian tradition for people who enjoy worshiping in a forest or on a mountain top—"God's handiwork"—
because they want to encounter the beauty of God in the natural
world. It is not a desire to be scorned, especially if the encounter with
such natural grace leads people to give thanks to the One who sustains the natural world with "greening power." As many Christians
have pointed out, however, the trouble with encountering God solely
through the natural world is that one will find it difficult to discover
Jesus of Nazareth. Even though reflection on the natural world may
lead one to conclude that God enjoys a richly diverse biosphere, it will
not necessarily communicate God's self-giving, embodied love for the
world. That God desires the liberation of all creation from the
oppressive power of evil will not necessarily be revealed by gazing on
tulips, lovely creatures that they are.

Thus Jews and Christians claim that God also reveals something of
God's character and intentions to and through people, ordinary people who communicate in word and deed. When my students ask,
"How does God communicate with humans?" I point them to this
medieval Christian adage: God communicates with people in ways in

which they can receive that communication, through words and actions. When the Bible narrates God communicating with Abraham, one assumes that such a communication took place in a language understandable to the surprised listener. When the Hebrews complained of thirst in the desert, the author of Exodus notes that they received fresh water from the rock rather than salty seawater. Of course, this process doesn't mean that the one receiving the communication will necessarily *understand* everything in the communication or its significance. No wonder one encounters so many diverse interpretations among Christians as to what constitutes the central insights of Christianity! Receiving a communication and understanding it are two different things. Ask any parent or teacher. Nonetheless, most Christians would agree that God communicates through persons and events, through word and action, to which the Bible is the preeminent witness.

Then, the encounter with God does not take place in a vacuum, in some spiritualized, ethereal cyberspace. Again and again and again, the biblical witness points to the real things of this earth and human experience as the ordinary means through which this remarkable communication occurs. What we know of God's existence and God's intentions toward the creation is, thus, *mediated* through ordinary experience (which may not seem ordinary at all). To claim that God's intentions for the creation are "mediated" through ordinary experience suggests that God takes human life seriously. It may also suggest that one might want to keep eyes, ears, and hands open, and take daily experience seriously, for it is in and through such mundane experience that God seems to want to disclose God's life and intentions.

God cannot be trapped or confined by the limitations of human communication and understanding, and so God can reveal God's self to anyone and in any way that God chooses to do so. Yet Christians hold that God's communication to and through Abraham and Sarah and their descendents, the people of Israel, and through Jesus of

Nazareth and his first followers, constitutes the central and foundational "revelation" in which Christianity is rooted. Without these persons and events, Christian faith would not exist.

Encountering God with food and drink

One of the fundamental claims of the faith is that God speaks and acts in order to create and sustain life. What God brings to birth, said Ambrose of Milan, the early Christian bishop, God nourishes with food and drink. The Bible narrates a voice speaking to Abraham, "Go from your country . . . to the land that I will show you" (Gen. 12:1), yet God also shares a meal with Abraham and Sarah. The voice in the burning bush tells Moses to lead the Hebrew people out of slavery (Exod. 3:9-10), yet before and after the departure from Egypt food and drink abound. The LORD calls Isaiah to speak judgment against the people of Judah (Isa. 6:1-9), yet promises them a banquet of rich food and well-aged wines. The lowly shepherd Amos denounces the wealthy who rob the poor of food (6:1-7), yet envisions a day when God will provide fruitful vineyards and abundant grain for all who are hungry and thirsty.

People use a variety of approaches in their reading of the Bible, this collection of diverse writings that have nourished and challenged the imagination of Jews and Christians for centuries. Some people hope to find comfort while others look for ethical models on which to pattern their lives. Some see the book as revealing God's promises while others believe that it communicates God's love for the human community. Here is another way one might consider reading and understanding the Bible: as the chronicle of the human encounter with God through food and drink. After all, the Bible begins with the offer of free food (Gen. 2:16) and the eating of forbidden fruit (Gen. 3:1-7) and ends with a fruit tree large enough to feed the hungry people of many nations that stream into the New Jerusalem (Rev. 22:14).

It should come as no surprise, then, that as contemporary Christians gather at table, they would hear the recital of new beginnings:

> We praise you for the grace shown to Israel,
> your chosen, the people of your promise:
> the rescue from Egypt,
> the gift of the promised land,
> the memory of the ancestors,
> the homecoming from exile,
> and the prophets' words that will not be in vain.
> (*With One Voice*, p. 23)

In each allusion to an event, promise, or people, however, can be found the memory of food and drink, a combination of words and actions through which something is disclosed about the significance of eating and drinking in the presence of God.

Consider, for instance, the encounter of Abraham and Sarah with three unexpected visitors (Gen. 18:1-15). In typical mideastern fashion, they welcome the three strangers with water for washing and the offer of bread to sustain them on their journey. They do not hide themselves or pretend that they have no food. What they actually prepare, however, is anything but a snack. Rather they offer a feast of freshly baked bread, milk, cheese, and roasted meat. Indeed, Abraham and Sarah become the servants of the meal they openly share with a group of men they think will soon be on their way. What they discover, much to their surprise, is that God has come to eat with them and promise the birth of a much longed-for child to an elderly couple seemingly past their fertility. The remarkable promise of life emerging in the womb mirrors the promise of life in the meal. But, of course, the great irony is that in their desire to be hospitable to strangers, Abraham and Sarah receive something far greater than they could have imagined: the hospitality of God. Although the biblical tradition will speak of God as powerful and even terrifying, here one sees the hospitality of God who shares food and drink with an elderly couple.

From this surprising pregnancy and birth issue a series of narratives in which food and drink figure prominently: Jacob receives Isaac's blessing as he offers him an aromatic stew (Gen. 27); Jacob's son Joseph saves Egypt during famine by carefully managing food stores (Gen. 41); he offers grain and thus the possibility of life to his brothers (Gen. 42–47) who then settle in Egypt. Scholars know today that among the earliest memories captured in the Hebrew Bible is that of the exodus from slavery under Pharaoh. Indeed, the passage from enslavement to freedom stands as the foundational event in the communal identity of the Jews: God reveals that God desires the liberation of God's people from the oppression of servitude. And the plagues that assail the oppressors strike primarily at their sources of food and drink: blood in the water; frogs, gnats, flies, and locusts ruining the food supply; disease in the livestock. Not unlike famine, the destruction of food and water supplies was understood as a sign of divine judgment. Where there is ample food and drink, there is salvation, wholeness, health, life.

Thus, when the Hebrew people at last depart from Egypt, they are commanded by God to keep the meal of their liberation each year as a perpetual memorial of God's mercy (Exod. 12). The keeping of Passover, then, becomes the means through which the people eat and drink the story of liberation from slavery. The eating and drinking of the story sets forth what God does for the people. But that same eating and drinking becomes the people's assent to their own identity and their mission to keep alive the revelation that God desires freedom for the creation. Even in the midst of bitter complaint and the ever-present yearning for the food available to slaves (Num. 11:1-1), God provides water, meat, and bread to this nomadic people on their journey to a land flowing with milk and honey.

The trouble is that the "memory of the ancestors" can be forgotten by successive generations who take for granted the abundance around them. Ahab and Jezebel, the wealthy rulers of Israel, had no qualms about illegally stealing the vineyard of Naboth. The prophet Elijah, himself a recipient of God's hospitality at the Wadi Cherith and the meager yet miraculous provisions of a widow in Zarephath (1 Kings 17), announced to Ahab that he would be consumed—eaten up—by the LORD (1 Kings 21) because he had recklessly "eaten up" the livelihood and family lands of poor Naboth. Even though the Hebrew Bible suggests that ample food and drink are a sign of God's salvific intentions, the willful deprivation of food brings God's condemnation. No wonder that later Jewish commentaries on the Bible would interpret the prohibition against murder in the Ten Commandments not only as the violent destruction of life but also as the failure to feed hungry people: one a quick, the other a slow death. That is an arresting interpretation, that the one who does not aid a hungry neighbor commits murder.

It thus appears that one of the primary functions of a prophet is to remind people of what they have forgotten. Whether such forgetfulness is conscious or unconscious, one may only guess. But it would seem that the prophetic voice in Israel's history speaks to the effects and social consequences of such forgetting. Although the annual celebration of the Passover meal was intended to shape the collective imagination of Israel as a people liberated by God from oppression and brought to a land flowing with milk and honey, the sad but almost predictable history of that nation or any other bears the marks of amnesia: the oppressed become the oppressors.

> Help, O LORD, for there is no longer anyone who is godly;
> the faithful have disappeared from humankind.
> They utter lies to each other; with flattering lips and a double
> heart they speak.

> May the LORD cut off all flattering lips, the tongue that makes
>   great boasts,
> those who say, "With our tongues we will prevail; our lips are
>   our own—who is our master?"
> "Because the poor are despoiled, because the needy groan, I will
>   now rise up," says the LORD;
> "I will place them in the safety for which they long."
> The promises of the LORD are promises that are pure, silver
>   refined in a furnace on the ground, purified seven times.
> You, O LORD, will protect us; you will guard us from this gener-
>   ation forever.
> (Ps. 12:1-7)

In a time of unprecedented national economic prosperity and ter-
ritorial expansion during the eighth century, the prophet Amos, himself a poor shepherd from Judah, traveled north to the kingdom of
Israel there to denounce the wealthy who not only overlooked the
needs of the poor and hungry people in their midst but also illicitly
manipulated debt and credit to gain even more wealth and land.
These were people who drank fine wines paid for with the exorbitant
interest charged on loans to the poor, a practice that only ensured
continued impoverishment (2:6-8). Amos knew that these people
worshiped on a regular basis. They believed themselves to be faithful
and religious people; they brought "thank offerings of leavened
bread" to God, yet they "oppressed the poor and crushed the needy"
(4:1-6). The wealthy elite hoarded food and drink, the gift of God to
all people, while the many poor went hungry in the streets.

What does God, the savior of Israel, ask from the people who have
forgotten the meaning of the meal of liberation celebrated at
Passover? "Let justice roll down like waters and righteousness like an
ever-flowing stream" (7:24). What God reveals or discloses is God's
desire for a just distribution or equitable access to food and drink for
all people. When food and drink are shared equitably, God's favor

rests on the people. Then "the prophets' words will not be in vain." Indeed, Amos ended his indictment of Israel with the promise of plentitude: "I will restore the fortunes of my people Israel, and they shall rebuild the ruined cities and inhabit them; they shall plant vineyards and drink their wine, and they shall make gardens and eat their fruit" (9:14). As in the vision of Isaiah (25:6-8), God serves as host at a feast to which everyone is welcome and there is no charge for "rich food" and "well-aged wines."

Giving thanks at table

God offers hospitality, liberation from oppression, food and drink for all people. In the biblical tradition and in the practice of Jews and Christians, the most appropriate response to the gift of broad fields and growing vineyards, to a land flowing with milk and honey, to enough food on the table for everyone is, quite simply, thanksgiving. Thank you. "It is right to give thanks and praise." The act of thanksgiving, of course, assumes the presence of something for which one is thankful, a motive for thanks. Thus, the act of thanksgiving presumes that something has been done, or said, or offered; someone acted or something occurred prior to the thanksgiving. Indeed, we find at the time of Jesus that Jewish table practice in the home invited the head of the household to bless God or give thanks to God for whatever was placed on the table, whether it be a simple meal of bread, meat, and wine or a table groaning with banquet foods in many courses. Before all else, before the eating and the drinking, words of blessing and thanksgiving were to be spoken or sung as the framework for the entire meal.

> You are blessed, LORD our God,
> Ruler of the universe,
> you who created the fruit of the vine.
> You are blessed, LORD our God,
> Ruler of the universe,
> you who have brought bread forth from the earth.

Such a simple blessing, said while holding bread or a cup of wine, contains a number of significant meanings. First, God is recognized and blessed. That, in and of itself, is a remarkable affirmation: there is more to the world than me or us. Set next to this household is the One who brings its very life into existence. And, of course, in that blessing is the recognition that humans are not self-made persons, a very un-American notion. With the whole creation, human existence flows from Another. If anything, such an affirmation could lead one to recognize that humans do not invent themselves but draw their existence from many others. Second, the meal is taken in the presence of God as if God were the host of the meal, the food and drink offered by God to those who are hungry and thirsty. Third, God is recognized as the ruler or creator—not only of the individual, the community, or the nation—but of the universe. Consider the confession in its social context. Various entities may claim to "rule" one's life: the emperor, the chieftain, the monarch, the majority, the boss, the religious leader, the spouse, the head of the household. The blessing of God signals, however, that no other creature can rightfully claim the ultimate allegiance of another. This God, who is free and transcends the many little rulers of human life, is named as the only One to whom blessing is given. So while the words affirm God as the one ruler, it also critiques the human desire to "rule" over others. Fourth, the bread or the cup or the meal is obviously the fruit of the earth and the work of human labor. Really? Placed next to these "earthly creations" is the recognition that God is the ultimate source of all life. If these good things ultimately come from God as free gifts, who are humans to hoard or waste them?

> We give you thanks, LORD our God,
> for you have given us for our inheritance
> a desirable land, that we may eat of its fruits
> and be filled with its goodness.

You are blessed, LORD our God,
for the land and the food.

It goes without saying that biblical Judaism doesn't appear to spend much time thinking about the afterlife or escaping this world. God's presence is a presence for this creation, for humans on this earth. God offers life here and now and that life, considered a blessing from God, is clearly earthy. Thus, Jewish blessing yields to thanksgiving for this land and this food and the goodness contained therein. Indeed, it was only when significant segments of early Christianity welcomed the spiritualizing tendencies of Greek and gnostic thought that the Jewish origins of Christianity were almost overwhelmed. The gnostic view affirmed an immortal, good, and immaterial soul and scorned a mortal, corrupt, and earthly body. The soul or mind, filled with the knowledge (gnosis) of God, would lead at death to a dematerialized existence. In contrast, the Jewish view affirmed an essential unity of body and spirit and humanity's connection to the earth and all other creatures. All of the creation was good, not just the invisible God or the intangible spirit. Consequently, two conflicting views emerged in Christianity regarding the creation. On the one hand, the Greek or gnostic tendency viewed the material creation as a prison to be escaped at death. The insignificant body, made of matter, molded from the soil of this earth, was considered insignificant if not imprisoning while the immortal soul or "enlightened" mind was extolled. On the other hand, the creation-affirming claims of Judaism remained alive for numbers of early Christians: God never intended an "escape" from what God has created, but its liberation from evil and its renewal by God's grace. A Christian influenced by the Jewish origins of Christianity wouldn't find it at all unusual to pray the following prayer, but I imagine it would be fairly difficult for a gnostic Christian to respond with a clear Amen:

God of all creation,
all you have made is good,
and your love endures forever.
You bring forth bread from the earth
and fruit from the vine.
Nourish us with these gifts,
that we might be for the world
signs of your gracious presence
in Jesus Christ our Lord.
(RW6, p. 56)

In the earliest biblical account of the Lord's supper, Paul relates to the early Christian community at Corinth the tradition he received from the Lord who took a loaf of bread, gave thanks, broke it and said, "This is my body for you"(1 Cor. 11:23-24). Paul the Jew knew the table practice of first-century Judaism: set next to the broad fields and fruitful vineyards of the good land, the household gives thanks for the hospitality of God, for the ongoing promise of liberation from servitude, for the food and drink that are given for the many, not just the few. Eat the bread, drink deeply from the wine cup, and one both tastes and sees the goodness of God (Ps. 34:8).

For reflection and discussion

1. If you accept the notion that the natural world is a living gift continually offered by God, what do you think is revealed through the natural world about God that would lead one to offer thanks?

2. People read the Bible in different ways. Some look for history, ethical guidelines, promises, or community, among other things. Why not study two or three texts that deal with food and hunger in order to discern what they reveal about the encounter between God

and humanity? Begin with Leviticus 19:1-2, 9-18; Ruth; and Isaiah 58:1-9a—all of which appear in the lectionary.

3. The Passover meal is one great thanksgiving to God for liberation from slavery, formation as a community, the gift of the Law, food and drink on the journey, and entrance into a land flowing with "milk and honey." In the Passover, our Jewish sisters and brothers eat and drink this story of Jewish identity and purpose. What might the study of the Passover meal's texts and actions reveal about God and God's intentions for humanity?

4. Study one or two thanksgiving prayers in *Lutheran Book of Worship, With One Voice,* or *Holy Communion and Related Rites* (Renewing Worship, vol. 6) to discover the ancient Jewish pattern of prayer: naming God, confessing the motive for thanksgiving to God, and asking God to act in a similar way today. What are the motives for thanksgiving in these worship texts?

5. Jews and Christians confess that God acts in history to create new possibilities and redeem what is held in bondage. As you think about the events of recent history throughout the world, what prompts you to offer thanksgiving?

3
Breaking Bread with the Outcast

At work in the house of study

"When I was a child, I spoke like a child, I thought like a child, I reasoned like a child" (1 Cor. 13:11a). When I was a child, I imagined that Jesus was my friend, he lived in both heaven and my heart at the same time; he protected me from a God who could become quite angry about my sins. I imagined that God could see everything I did and knew every thought I was thinking, every second of the day. From the paintings and pictures in our church and textbooks, I knew that Jesus looked much like me: he had pale skin and brown hair. His eyes, however, looked more like my dad's: they were blue. Though Jesus and I wore different clothing, I was familiar with long, white robes and could see the similarity between pastors and the great shepherd of the flock. I couldn't tell if he was poor or wealthy but he seemed to like children and people who had made a mess of their lives. I knew that Jesus came to this earth from outer space (i.e., heaven) for one purpose: to die so that God would forgive my sins and welcome me into heaven where I would never be separated from my family. Thus, the thoughts of a young boy about Jesus of Nazareth.

"When I became an adult, I put an end to childish ways" (1 Cor. 13:11b). This shift in thinking is not to say that as I grew older I no longer believed Jesus to be friendly or that my sense of sin evaporated upon entering adolescence or college. Having experienced my parents' forgiveness, I came to recognize that to forgive another person was, in fact, one of the most difficult things to do and that many people rarely experience it. After all, revenge is so much easier, isn't it? Yet in that movement from "I reasoned like a child" to "when I became an adult," my understanding of Jesus of Nazareth—his person, context, and message—shifted and was shaped by that most liberating and dangerous of things: ordinary study.

I think anyone is fortunate who grows up in a home where study and learning are considered allies in thinking about God or faith or the church, rather than its enemies. Without ever using that phrase coined by Anselm of Canterbury—"faith seeking understanding"—my parents knew that study led to a deeper and more mature understanding of a life lived from the perspective of the Christian faith. But one must grow into it. To paraphrase Gail Ramshaw, the child in each of us may be drawn to the story of Jesus' birth in Bethlehem read from Luke's gospel at every Christmas Eve liturgy (2:1-14); it is the thoughtful adult, however, who will need to grapple with the meaning of "the Word became flesh" as read from the Gospel of John on Christmas Day (1:1-14). I tell my students that they would be surprised if I confessed to them in all seriousness that I believed Santa Claus existed or that little red horned demons breathed sickness into people. Surrounded by mature adults, a child has the freedom to entertain such magical notions. But such thinking will not be of much use to the adult who needs to face the harsh realities, unsolved riddles, and seemingly capricious turns of life with both wisdom and courage.

Under the watchful guidance of university pastors, college professors, and graduate school mentors, I came to understand that Jesus did not look like me. He was not a Nordic god but a first century Palestinian Jew who lived under the oppressive regime of Roman military occupation. He spoke, thought, and acted as a Jew, a man who may have been an artisan but was much closer socioeconomically to impoverished peasants than first-century wealthy elites in Jerusalem or twenty-first-century middle-class Christians in North America. I also came to recognize that the forgiveness of sins was not the primary message of Jesus but rather his proclamation in word and deed of the coming reign or "rule" of God in first-century Roman Palestine. The earliest gospel points to this central image in his public life: "Jesus came to Galilee, proclaiming the good news of God, and saying, 'The time is fulfilled, and the kingdom of God has come near; repent, and believe in the good news'"(Mark 1:14-15). The rest of the gospel is the good news of how that reign of God is coming near in human life and history through word and deed. Clearly one significant mark of God's reign in human life *is* forgiveness or reconciliation but, to quote Paul who gives one of the briefest definitions of the "reign of God" in the New Testament, where God is there is also "justice, peace, and joy in the Spirit" (Rom. 14:17).

Such study, undertaken among faithful and inquisitive Christian scholars, revealed the Jewishness of Jesus, his deeply Jewish proclamation of the nearness of the reign of God, and his consistent invocation of God rather than himself. These days, such insights are recognized by some and overlooked by others. If Jesus' proclamation in word and deed pointed to God's just and peaceful reign in human life and history, then might it not follow that his disciples are also called to serve that reign of God, albeit as discerned in Jesus of Nazareth? From this view, the function of the church is not to maintain itself but to serve the reign of God as revealed by Jesus of Nazareth. In a consumer culture such as North America, however, it is easy to imagine these days that the church's purpose is to order its life around sustaining or "growing" churches rather than serving the reign of God's justice and peace. But we have to ask: was Jesus executed because he wanted to "grow" a worldwide organization (or as some might say, a "gospel community") or because his understanding of the reign of God proved too troubling for those who claimed to "rule" or "reign" over his land and people?

Blessed are they who eat bread in the kingdom

As a child growing up in a church that faithfully kept the liturgical calendar, we were constantly entering into the life of Jesus through the feasts and seasons of the year. Of course, the incarnation (Christmas) and the resurrection (Easter) figured prominently in the life of the church. As children, we almost knew by heart Luke's story of the birth and John's story of the last supper, death, and resurrection. Each Sunday we received the body and blood of Christ for the forgiveness of our sins, linking us to the last supper Jesus kept with his disciples "on the night in which he was betrayed" (Matt. 26:26-29). These practices made it clear that the reason for the birth (celebrated at Christmas) was the death (celebrated on Good Friday) that won the forgiveness communicated regularly through communion (celebrated every Sunday), in what was called "the weekly celebration of the resurrection."

Patient study, however, can lead to a difficult awareness: what we take for granted as *the* model of life or ethics or faith may not be the only one around. Here's an example. For many Christians, the communion they celebrate on Sunday focuses on one supper that Jesus shared toward the end of his life as narrated in the three gospels of Mark, Matthew, and Luke (interestingly enough, John has a supper but the action remembered is washing feet, not breaking bread). When a biblical scholar led us in a study of the *other* meals of Jesus, we discovered previously unknown riches. It went something like this: if the primary proclamation of Jesus was the nearness of God's reign of justice, peace, and joy, (1) what do the meals of Jesus reveal about his understanding of the reign of God? (2) what was the social context in which Jesus kept these "meals of the kingdom"? and (3) why would such an enacted proclamation lead him into trouble and eventually to his death?

In narrating the first public meal of Jesus, Mark notes that he kept company with a tax collector and "sinners" (2:13-17). Given that a tax collector was an employee of the Roman occupation force, Jesus could not have been perceived as a "patriotic" citizen who shunned the "traitors" of his own people, but as someone who would welcome the hospitality of someone perceived by others as collaborator with the enemy, an "outcast." Indeed, as biblical scholars have made clear in the last twenty years, the term *sinner* in first-century Palestine did not apply to all humanity as later Christian theology would claim, but to persons who were considered nonobservant Jews, chronically sick, mentally disturbed, impoverished and thus unable to pay the religious tax to the Temple or tax to the Romans, engaged in work which to observant people made them look religiously "impure" (e.g., morticians and prostitutes), and gentiles (thus Romans and Greeks). The question asked by the religiously observant who watched Jesus is quite logical: "Why does he eat with tax collectors and sinners?" In other words, why does a seemingly observant Jew share bread and thus life with people on the margins of religion and society? Could it be that the "religiously observant" view of life in the presence of God was wrong, that the nearness of God could not be limited by the religious standards of the status quo? By sharing meals with tax collectors, prostitutes, and unethical rascals, working for food on the Sabbath, and directing his followers to welcome the chronically sick and mentally disturbed to their meals, was Jesus not revealing the hospitality of God that seemingly knows no limitations? Indeed, it became clearer to us as we studied the meals of Jesus that his presence as guest or host had a transforming effect on those who were at the same meal. Such meals revealed a "contrast" experience between

God's open and inclusive "reign" and the oppressive "reign" of the Roman emperor and his wealthy Palestinian collaborators. In other words, Jesus had crossed the boundary between "who's in" and "who's out" that marks every group or society of the first or twenty-first century.

Mark narrates another meal that Jesus keeps, this time not with a few tax collectors or "sinners" but with what scholars consider a large crowd of hungry peasants (6:30-44). Read carefully, one recognizes that this meal takes place in a deserted place, oddly reminiscent of God's feeding of the Hebrew people in the Sinai wilderness through Moses (Exod. 16) and Elijah being fed in time of famine (1 Kings 17). The disciples want to send the crowds away to buy their own food to eat. Read in its social and historical context, in a land suffering economic oppression and military occupation, the disciples were asking the impossible of people who no longer could rely on their own labor to feed them. Controlled by wealthy landowners and military occupiers, food sources were limited. Here the economically marginal and thus impoverished crowd was looking for what their own history has told them *God* provides: a just and equitable sharing of the fruits of field and vine. That Jesus provides more than enough bread and fish for them to eat not only serves as a sign of God's desire that there be equitable sharing from God's abundant earth but also God's particular regard for the poor. Here Jesus engages in the regular practice of the Jewish household: he first offers thanksgiving to God for the fruit of the field (bread) and the harvest of the sea (fish) and then distributes these "gifts of God" to the "people of God." But there is something startling in all of this: God is proclaimed in the thanksgiving as "ruler" of the earth, not the Roman emperor or the wealthy landowners who control the land and deprive the people of the land's abundance. Indeed, if Jesus takes the normal table practice *outdoors*, it is the poor who constitute the household! The kingdom or reign of God provides enough food and drink for all.

But, of course, we're left with that third question: Why would such an enacted proclamation lead Jesus into trouble and eventually to his death? The followers of Jesus, among them the New Testament writers, have answered that question in different ways over the past 2000 years. Here are a few of them. Jesus was arrested and crucified because (1) he claimed to be divine, one with God and God's only son, a blasphemous insult to Jews; (2) he usurped the sole right of God to forgive sin; (3) he created a new "gracious" faith discontinuous with the old "legalistic" faith into which he was born (so far the Jews are the culprits); (4) the Romans could not abide anyone under their rule who claimed to be a messiah or a king; (5) Jesus' growing popularity with "the rabble" threatened the fragile order needed for the peaceful celebration of Passover (the Romans are the culprits). Each answer has enjoyed greater or lesser popularity in the history of Christianity.

What about this one? Jesus was arrested and crucified because throughout his public life, in word and deed, he proclaimed God as ruler and the nearness of God's reign of justice, peace, and joy to his own people. "The Spirit of the Lord is upon me," announces the Lucan Jesus, quoting from Isaiah, "because he has anointed me to bring good news to the poor. He has sent me to proclaim release to the captives and recovery of sight to the blind, to let the oppressed go free, to proclaim the year of the Lord's favor" (Luke 4:18-19). If, for instance, in a society where the few grew wealthy off the labor of the impoverished many and enforced that crushing labor through military force, wouldn't the proclamation of a God who offers a new Passover to another kind of life be deeply threatening to the powerful few? If, in a society where the many poor were thought to be "unholy" or "unworthy" or "impure," at a distance from a "holy" God, wouldn't eating and drinking with this One who proclaimed God's inclusive and merciful presence to all people be astonishingly attractive? In a society where the many had limited or no access to God's abundant food for themselves and their children, wouldn't the proclamation of a reign in which such food and drink were available to everyone alarm those who did not recognize or scorned the promises of God to sustain all life that comes from God?

As study continued, it became clearer that Jesus' profound theological vision of life lived in the presence of a gracious and merciful God possessed economic, social, and political implications. Is it any wonder, then, that Jesus was arrested and crucified during the feast of Passover, that great celebration of *God* who liberates God's people from the oppressive powers of evil that deform, crush, or abuse the very life God created to flourish in peace and joy? Is it any wonder that he was crucified by the Romans who could not abide a "kingdom of justice and peace" so at odds with an empire built on greed and military force? Is it any wonder, then, that one hears today such hope for a "passing over" into this reign of God voiced in images drawn from the New Testament and the struggle to liberate slaves?

> God of our weary years, God of our silent tears . . .
> The cry of the poor has become your own cry;
> our hunger and thirst for justice is your own desire.
> In the fullness of time, you sent your chosen servant
> to preach good news to the afflicted,
> to break bread with the outcast and despised,
> and to ransom those in bondage to prejudice and sin.
> (RW6, p. 70)

Broken and poured out for many

To say the least, study began to shift our thinking not only about the Lord's supper but also about revelation. What is it that God is revealing in Jesus of Nazareth and thus disclosing for those who claim to be his followers "sealed with the Spirit and marked with the cross of Christ"? While much conventional thinking among Christians suggests that people must do or believe something in order to be "right" with God, or that being Christian is a deeply personal and "spiritual" matter, or that the primary function of Christianity is to ensure one's individual immortality, study can lead one to consider other possibilities. Could it be, for instance, that God is revealing God's continuous desire to come toward God's creation, to liberate humans from greed and abuse, from the evil that crushes the poor and excludes the seemingly "unworthy," and to thrust Christians into the world as responsible adults, capable of cooperating with these intentions in the economic, political, and social dimensions that shape life in the world? If so, one could say, then, that Christianity's purpose is not so much about drawing people into church as *sending them forth* into the world as servants of God's reign of "justice, peace, and joy." To follow the pattern of the Lord's supper, one might say that God is pouring out God's life for the world as food and drink for the hungry, the poor, the afflicted, the outcast and despised who have no hope except in God and God's servants. If so, is it not possible to affirm that Jesus of Nazareth is the embodiment of that outpouring, now given in bread broken and wine poured?

In his reflection on the mystery the crucified and risen Christ, Paul quotes from a hymn already being sung at Christian gatherings in the early first century: "Christ Jesus . . . emptied himself, taking the form of a slave, being born in human likeness. And being found in human form, he humbled himself and became obedient to the point of death—even death on a cross" (Phil. 2:7-8). One should not glide over the first four words too quickly—Christ Jesus emptied himself—for they bear a striking resemblance to the ordinary action of pouring wine or water out of a pitcher. As a young boy I thought of Jesus as a Nordic god and my personal friend, reigning in the heavens above the earth, who would help me get to a new place after death. The gift of communion was the forgiveness that held the promise of my immortality. For a young boy, "God in the heavens" and "my personal friend" were powerful symbols that elicited both awe and a measure of smugness; after all, I knew that I "possessed" what many other people did not. What I had not yet considered was the meaning or significance of the action I saw and participated in every Sunday, that breaking of bread and pouring of wine.

For bread to be eaten, it must be broken. The size and power of the large loaf is too much for anyone to place in the mouth: it would suffocate or choke them. The same goes, however, for powerful ideas, symbols, words, and rituals in every dimension of life. They must be "broken," that is, criticized or challenged so that they do not become gods unto themselves. This is to suggest that such powerful things, including the ones we cherish the most, hold the power to overwhelm and choke the life out of the very thing they are supposed to nourish. For instance, I once took a class with a professor who let it be known that he was the expert and we students were know-nothings. Indeed, he would entertain few if any questions. The course, in effect, became an exercise in "bowing" or submitting to his ego if one expected to pass the class. He held on to his knowledge—his power—to impress us rather than to give it away in authentic teaching. He believed his ideas and his knowledge were "powerful" but could not share such things with us in any meaningful way. His "power" was not "broken" or criticized by himself or anyone else.

Indeed, the smugness that accompanied the symbol of "Jesus as my personal friend" needed to be broken by the awareness of the One who pours out life for the many, including those who have no recourse to the words and supper of Christians.

Paul engages in such breaking, such criticism when he says, "Christ Jesus emptied himself." One would normally expect a god, the son of a god, or the anointed agent of a god to appear with power that shocks and awes. The striking thing is that in their history, Christians have readily accepted such conventional thinking by the use of royal or military language in far too many sermons, prayers, and songs with the sole purpose of impressing humans with nothing less than the "almighty" and "majestic" power of God, Jesus, or the church. But here is the great irony: for Paul, God reveals God's self in a first-century Palestinian peasant. That is, the power of God—which one could easily imagine is sufficient enough to dazzle even the most hardened atheist and make the very rocks scream out—is broken apart and given away, poured out, for anyone who needs it. In the "kingdom of Rome" or any other empire, power is exercised over "subjects" not only to impress but also to terrify into submission. How odd it is, then, that such power is challenged by the One who proclaims an alternative reign where power is used to welcome, enlighten, and nourish. "Then he poured water into a basin and began to wash the disciples' feet and to wipe them with the towel that was tied around him." (John 13:5). Washing feet, to say the least, is not the action of a Nordic god.

If, as many Christians claim with the Emmaus disciples, Christ is recognized in the breaking of the bread, is not God's power and presence always being broken and poured out freely for the life of the world? "For God so loved the world," wrote John, not just for me or my church or my nation but the cosmos. If the shape of that giving is cruciform, and that giving is for the life of the world, is not the reign of God intended to inundate every form of suffering with the promise of God's own justice, peace, and joy? Here the gift of communion is the promise of a dynamic presence in, with, and under this life, since "neither death nor life, nor things present, nor things to come . . . will be able to separate us from the love of God in Christ Jesus" (Rom. 8:38-39).

What is the gift of this supper? In the world in which we live, the strong continue to crush the weak for economic, political, psychological, or religious advantage. Is it not possible that this supper offers an alternative: that the "strong" might pour out their power to ensure that the "weak" actually survive and flourish? Who knows but that a joyous murmur might escape the lips of those who never imagined it possible.

For reflection and discussion

1. The Lutheran reform movement emerged out of a university in which Luther and his colleagues both studied and asked troubling questions in their time. It is one legacy of the Lutheran reform. When has study of God, humanity, or the world expanded or deepened your experience of faith?

2. Describe what you think was your childhood understanding of Jesus of Nazareth. As you have grown older, how has that understanding changed?

3. Jesus' proclamation focused on the nearness of God's reign or "rule" in human life and history. Yet Christians have understood the reign or kingdom of God in different ways throughout their history. How would you describe the reign of God in human life and history today?

4. Luke 4:18-19 narrates one "mission" statement in the New Testament. The rest of Luke's gospel is good news for people who experience the presence of Jesus in their lives. If this statement were your congregation's "mission statement," how would the ministries of the congregation be ordered to extend that mission in your community?

5. Jesus was criticized for the company he kept at meals. Why do you think the Christian community is or is not criticized for its meal practice?

4

Pour Us Out
for Each Other

You, you're the only one

At the university where I teach, the student life office reports that one of the most difficult challenges facing first-year students is the need to share a room with another student in a residence hall. Growing up in homes where they had their own bedrooms, many of our students have no experience of sharing a television, a telephone, a closet, or a schedule with someone else. Walking across campus, one notes increasing numbers of students wearing headphones, listening to anything but the sound of the wind, the birds, the greetings of others. Please understand me. These are bright, friendly, and hardworking students who intend to pursue vocations of service in the world, young people who share a genuine commitment to the welfare of the global community. It's just that many if not most of them think they will be working on their own, by themselves, alone.

Years ago at a conference in Rome, I met a Dominican nun from South Africa. With other members of the conference, we took a day trip to the medieval hill town of Orvieto to view its splendid Gothic cathedral and taste its famous white wines. A convivial group of travelers, we enjoyed each other's company and fell into conversation easily. Given that the conference theme was on Christianity and world cultures, it wasn't long before we started talking about our respective cultures. "One of the greatest struggles in my land," said the South African, "is that people chatter so much they find it difficult to be silent and listen, truly listen." An American spoke up and said that one of the great challenges facing Christianity in North America is the overwhelming power of the "individual" and the corresponding loss of any sense of community. "Yes," said our South African friend who had studied in Chicago for a number of years, "how sad it is that your people think the journey must be walked alone." And there, in that brief conversation, African "community" met the American "individual."

The Berkeley sociologist Robert Bellah notes that one near fatal flaw in American religion has been the growing acceptance of a rigorous form of individualism derived from strains of Reformed and Radical Protestantism that found welcome ground in the soil of early American culture. It looks something like this: Where the relationship between God and the individual adult is the primary source of religious imagination, it has been and remains easier for the bonds of community to unravel whenever there is disagreement. In the end, as Bellah points out, you're left with a religion of one: one person and one God. Although a remarkable degree of religious diversity can be found in North America, much of it is due to the deep cultural code that places great value on individual choice and little value on the commonweal.

At the end of one study, Bellah concluded that most North Americans now understand religious affiliation normatively as a highly personal, private, and voluntary matter. In a "utilitarian" view of both life and religion, one joins and stays in a group only so long as it serves one's personal needs. Indeed, in a culture where ethnic identity no longer holds religious identity ("We're Swedish, so we're Lutheran"), religion is a matter of personal choice at the great buffet of religious diversity ("We're American, so we'll try religion X, Y, or

Z"). Such a cultural context proves challenging, to say the least, for those forms of Christianity that arise out of biblical, communal, and sacramental foundations. In the desire to be assimilated into North American culture, to be accepted and not scorned as aliens or strangers, Christians who trace their history, practice, and theology to such communal sensibilities are in for a struggle. Which will it be: a good American or a faithful Christian? For the most part, the tension has been relieved through the accommodation of Christianity as a religion of the individual, the adult individual.

The dark side of such a powerful cultural value is that the great American "I" weighs heavily in the collective unconscious. Many North Americans simply take it for granted that life is about my needs and me: "I want a bedroom for myself. I need my own cell phone. I expect to have a latte prepared just as I want it." No wonder that cultural formation in individualism makes it difficult for North American Christians to grasp the fundamental Christian affirmation that God is a community of three, a trinity of persons. When cultural individualism shapes the religious imagination, it can be easier for Christians to speak and sing about Jesus and only Jesus: "I have a personal relationship with the Lord. Faith is between God and me. I prefer a church that will meet my (very unique) needs." In a consumer culture, it is not difficult to imagine a congregation or parish as a spiritual grocery store with endless options available.

It would seem that as increasing numbers of mainline Christian denominations have waned in the latter days, some of their leaders have attempted to keep or gain members by acting as religious "entrepreneurs" who are willing to provide at least a modicum of diversified "services" to their congregational "clientele." And, thus, in the mixing of marketing techniques and religion, one has the uneasy alliance between consumerism and Christianity. It was with some trepidation that I recently listened as a very earnest minister explained the number of options available during the communion at his church: wheat bread, nonwheat bread, wafers; drinking from a common cup of wine or a common cup of grape juice; communion by dipping whatever kind of bread one had in wine or grape juice; standing or kneeling. Such variety, he added, was expanded by the possibility of attending a "traditional," "contemporary," "meditative," or "youth" service. "Ach so," said a friend from Germany who heard the list of options, "a little mini mart."

Broken for ya'll

In the midst of such well-meaning efforts to "individualize" Christian worship by developing a diverse array of options that are intended to respond to personal tastes, other Christians have become newly aware that they actually celebrate a common pattern of worship. In its ecumenical study on *Baptism, Eucharist, and Ministry*, the World Council of Churches pointed to a common order of worship shared by Christians as diverse as Bolivian Lutherans, Korean Presbyterians, Russian Orthodox Christians, Egyptian Copts, Polish Catholics, and South African Anglicans. Given the history of partisan fighting between Christian denominations since the sixteenth century, the degree of agreement on the pattern and its significance is astonishing. So just as many Christian communities in North America are diversifying their "worship program" to appeal to individual tastes, Christian communities through the world are beginning to recognize what they hold in common: "The sharing in one bread and the common cup in a given place demonstrates and effects the oneness of the sharers with Christ and with their fellow sharers in all times and places" (*Baptism, Eucharist and Ministry*, E19).

This common pattern of worship shared by diverse communities throughout the world offers Christians the opportunity to reflect on their common biblical, communal, and sacramental roots. But the words and actions of such a pattern also serve as a "remedial norm" that can critique cultural values when they appear to swamp the deeper meanings alive in the Christian communions. Consider, for instance, the words used in many Christian communities as they gather for worship: "The grace of our Lord Jesus Christ, the love of God, and the communion of the Holy Spirit be with you all." Of course the greeting is a direct quotation from Paul's second letter to the Corinthian Christians (2 Cor. 13:13). When Americans hear that "you" in English, however, they may actually hear "you and you alone." Yet the "our," "communion," and "you all" make it clear that the greeting is extended to a community, especially that "you all"— υμων in Greek—as if Paul were a Texan shouting out "Hey, ya'll!"

Or consider the words spoken during the thanksgiving over bread and cup: "The Lord Jesus on the night when he was betrayed took a loaf of bread, and when he had given thanks, he broke it and said, 'This is my body that is for you'" (1 Cor. 11:23-24). The leader of worship may say, "This is my body that is for you," but my American ears hear "for me." And Luther might agree: "Ponder and include yourself personally in the 'you' so that [Christ] may not speak to you in vain" (The Large Catechism, The Book of Concord, p. 173). Indeed, in many Christian communities, as the bread and cup are given to each person, the minister says, "given for you, shed for you," thus underscoring the personal reception of bread and cup. Yet the meaning of the original Greek won't let me stay too long with me: it is υμων—you all—that opens beyond the "me" to the "many," from the "I" to the "we." Once again, it is that annoying pebble in the comfortable shoe of individual consciousness: it is always about more than you alone or me alone.

To participate in the Holy Communion is to be drawn into something greater than the looming American "I." It is the invitation if not the challenge to recognize the communion one enjoys with others rather than the lonely self. Of course, communion begins with baptism, that most inclusive sacrament. As most but not all Christians teach, baptism is primarily an act of God, but the God who acts in baptism isn't a divine monad. The One who acts in baptism is a community of three diverse persons who continually create, save, and sustain all things. Indeed, the very act of baptism initiates one into the community of the Holy Three rather than an individual relationship with Jesus. But there is more. One of the most shocking claims made by Christians in the stratified society of the ancient Mediterranean world was that anyone is welcome into this baptismal "body," this table communion. To say the least, things get messy. Slaves and their masters are welcome along with women and men, children and the elderly, the sophisticated and the vulgar, hawks and doves, the wealthy and the poor, the thoughtful and the rash, superstitious people and rational people, as well as "Parthians, Medes, Elamites, and residents of Mesopotamia, Judea and Cappadocia, Pontus and Asia, Phrygia and Pamphylia, Egypt and the parts of Libya belonging to Cyrene, and visitors from Rome, both Jews and proselytes, Cretans and Arabs" (Acts 2:9-11), in other words people from just about every race and ethnic group of the known world. Believe me: a committee couldn't have come up with a better case for social disaster. With baptism, one enters into a community of sometimes heroic and sometimes timid, sometimes bold and sometimes intransigent people called "the body of Christ." To put it plainly: one receives both the community of the Trinity and this baptismal community at the same time, not one without the other. It's ya'll, not you and you alone.

A messy body

Thus, we find Paul writing to the fractious Christian community in Corinth, "The cup of blessing that we bless, is it not a sharing in the blood of Christ? The bread that we break, is it not a sharing in the body of Christ? Because there is one bread, we who are many are one body, for we all partake of the one bread" (1 Cor. 10:16-17). Why does he need to ask the question about communion? In ancient

Mediterranean cultures, modern Europe and Latin America, and most North American bakeries, bread is sold whole as one loaf. To eat the bread, it must be broken apart and then shared. From the one loaf, the many eat. Of course, that seems so obvious except for North Americans who buy presliced bread at a grocery store and receive prepunched individual wafers at communion. Paul is able to use the lively and rich metaphor of "sharing in the body of Christ" precisely because he is observing the bread-breaking practice of a bread-eating culture. The many, as it were, commune with the one Christ in the Holy Communion. But that one Christ calls a community, not a group of individuals, into existence through baptism and sustains that one "body" with one bread and one cup. For the past fifty years, pastors, teachers, bishops, theologians, and biblical scholars have encouraged Christians to return, in a rather countercultural manner, to the use of one bread broken and given to the many: not because they are antiquarians or want to subvert the profits going to companies that peddle presliced bread, but because Christianity itself is a deeply communal and diversely messy reality, the corporate "body of Christ" enlivened by the Spirit. The texts spoken and sung in the Christian liturgy witness to that surprising reality:

> Blessed be God who gives *us* life with all of creation
> In peace, let *us* pray to the Lord
> This is the feast of victory for *our* God
> *We* believe in one God
> Hear *our* prayer
> Peace be with *you all*
> It is right to give *our* thanks and praise
> Shed for *you* and for *all people*
> Give *us* this day *our* daily bread
> Grant *us* peace
> (RW6, pp. 6, 9, 10, 12, 13, 14, 16, 17, emphasis added)

Honestly, can you really imagine praying the Lord's Prayer with these words, "My Father in heaven"? No wonder the word *communion* (from the Latin "com-munere") means "a sharing of gifts." In this "holy" communion, the people receive the gifts of earth's broad fields, the many thanksgiving meals of Israel, the table fellowship of Jesus who ate with "the many," and participation in the body's one bread and one cup, the body and blood of Christ. "Enliven this bread, awaken this body," says one new thanksgiving prayer, "pour us out for each other" (RW6, p. 65). Perhaps most North American ears can receive "enliven" and "awaken." It is the "pouring out for each other" petition that might be the most difficult to imagine for this messy and sometimes quarrelsome body.

Well, Paul knew something about quarrelsome congregations that forgot or overlooked the open and inclusive meal practice of Jesus. While he commends the Christian community at Corinth because they maintain the traditions he has handed on to them (1 Cor. 11:2), he quickly reproves them for failing to discern the significance of the Lord's supper, as if to say: You received this from me concerning the supper of the Lord but you, in fact, do otherwise.

Now in the following instructions I do not commend you, because when you come together it is not for the better but for the worse. For, to begin with, when you come together as a church, I hear that there are divisions among you; and to some extent I believe it. . . . When you come together, it is not really to eat the Lord's supper. For when the time comes to eat, each of you goes ahead with your own supper, and one goes hungry and another becomes drunk. What! Do you not have homes to eat and drink in? Or do you show contempt for the church of God and humiliate those who have nothing? What should I say to you? Should I commend you? In this matter I do not commend you! (11:17-18, 20-22)

What is the "problem" in this Christian community? First, we hear reports of factions. In the increasingly polarized economic and political landscape of American life, such news should come as no surprise to anyone today. But when the Corinthian assembly gathers, "it is not really to eat the Lord's supper." Oh, of course, they are holding a supper, maybe even a religious meal of some kind. It's just not the *Lord's* supper. And it cannot be the Lord's supper because of the greed and disregard held by some for other members of the body. In this case, wealthy members with much to eat and drink who overlook the needs of the poor and hungry members have contradicted the practice of mutual sharing of gifts. Here the disparity between rich and poor, itself a growing reality in North American life, seems to have become a norm that pulls apart the one body whose life is nourished by the One broken and poured out for the many in his death. The Christian community, born in the inclusive waters of baptism and nourished as one body in the one bread broken and one cup poured, is intended to resist what is normative in most societies: the spirit of factionalism, of group interest, of the like minded clique.

Of course ancient and medieval societies were what anthropologists call "kinship societies," that is, societies in which the value of communal life and communal norms predominated over the individual and what modern people call "individual rights." Indeed, the Bible and 1500 years of Christian theology were written in the context of such kinship societies. Not until the fifteenth and sixteenth centuries, in European and North American contexts, do we see the emergence of the individual, walking away, as it were, from all those early Christian paintings and medieval frescos of the communion of saints covering the walls of just about every church and chapel. Even though the western focus on the inalienable rights of the individual is a relatively recent development in the history of humankind, one can rightly argue that it needed to be so, that the power of the group needed and needs to be criticized so that it does not crush the individual or silence the voice on the margins or in the minority. And it is in that context—resistance to the overwhelming power of a group that can seek to perpetuate its power in an unchanging status quo—that one needs to hear the voice of the German mystics who influenced Luther so profoundly. Faith, trust in God, grasps the "for me" addressed by Christ to the person. Indeed, one might argue that it was the Protestant reformers' clear insistence on Christ coming to the individual with grace and mercy that cultivated the soil in which the seeds of democracy would be planted and grow.

Yet we find in renaissance and reformation societies neither rejection of community nor the modern adulation of the self-sufficient individual that is often projected into the sixteenth and subsequent centuries. Rather one discovers both "community" and "individual" in healthy tension with each other, a necessary counterplay between the one voice and the many. The question that faces North American Christians who find their identity in the biblical, trinitarian, and sacramental treasures of the faith is whether cultural exaltation of the individual has overwhelmed the capacity to receive the gift of communion with Christ and *all* that Christ loves: this creation, humankind in all its riotous diversity, this whining and faithful pilgrim band called the church, the bodies that cry out for mercy.

"The gifts of God for the people of God," proclaims the presiding minister.

"The body of Christ, given for you," announces the communion minister.

The body born of Mary, one with humanity.

The body of the poor, welcomed to eat with Jesus.

The body healed freely, rejoicing in God's mercy.

The body broken in torture, its blood shed on the cross.

The body raised and transfigured, filling the world.

The body of this one bread, broken and eaten by the many.

The body of Christ, the baptized eating and drinking together.

The body of Christ, poured for the life of the world.

There is much in this body.

For reflection and discussion

1. Although many North Americans consider a cultural emphasis on the individual and individual rights both normal and sacred, what might be some of the harmful effects of such a strong cultural value?

2. The Bible and Christian worship speak of community and care for the common good, but North American culture tends to emphasize the individual and care for individual needs. Do you ever sense a conflict between the two in your life? If so, how does it manifest itself?

3. Describe, if you can, an experience of the Lord's supper in which you sensed a bond or communion with other Christians.

4. The texts and songs that surround the Holy Communion speak repeatedly of a common sharing in the one bread and one cup. What is gained by such a biblical focus on communion with each other in a culture of individualism?

5. It may be worthwhile to read *What are the essentials of Christian worship?* by Gordon Lathrop, Lutheran professor of worship in Philadelphia (see the bibliography). Written for congregational study and reflection, the author points to what Christians hold as essential in worship and why such matters are essential for Christian communities.

5
Have Mercy on Us

When human bonds are broken

The front page of the newspaper reports the following stories: the murder of a homeless man by a white supremacist, the deaths of seven U.S. soldiers in Iraq, a march commemorating the Tiananmen Square massacre, a charge against the United States for allegedly committing war crimes, the unsolved mystery of fifteen dog poisonings in the city, and the failure of two large manufacturers to regulate the toxins they pour into the bay. When I read the reports and ask my students why life seems to be marked by such unrelieved suffering, they propose a variety of causes. Ignorance is big on the list and thus could be remedied with more education. The alleviation of oppressive socioeconomic conditions that influence human behavior would help. A few voices shout out "Politicians!" "Government!" "Lobbyists!"

Others think that inattentive parents and teachers contribute to "social" problems. Remember, this generation of college students has been through high school "lockdown" drills in the wake of the Columbine shootings in 1999. Indeed, many of them do not believe that North America is a safe place to live. To say the least, the events of September 11, national terror alerts, and two military conflicts abroad serve as potent signs of insecurity in the world. Of course, it doesn't help that recent film releases include a cataclysmic earthquake, the explosion of earth's core, the destruction of cities due to global warming, deadly conspiracies in government and religion, and the final battle between good and evil at Armageddon. The Cold War ended, everyone breathed a collective sigh of relief, only to wake up to global terror networks here and abroad. Perhaps we see some truth in Anne Frank's conviction, steadfastly maintained as she and her Jewish family hid from the Nazis in an Amsterdam attic, that people are, at heart, basically good. Many of my students would like to believe it, but we see little evidence, at least in the media, that such may be true.

A dean at the university where I teach once floated the idea that we all share a common ethical vision. I don't doubt for one second that most if not all of my colleagues claim an ethical vision or norm. Indeed, many of them engage their students in the study of the most pressing economic, medical, environmental, legal, educational, and racial crises facing humankind. I'm just not sure that we share a "common" ethical vision, especially if it means the cause of such crises rests *solely* in "dominant society," "hierarchical," "patriarchal," or "post-colonial" social systems. Although Europeans and North Americans are quick to claim the inalienable rights of the individual and equally quick to criticize groups (e.g., government, churches, multinational corporations, administrators, the U.N.), some difficulty arises with the claim that individuals, including us, may contribute to the suffering of the world.

Not unlike most of our students, we are influenced by pieces of a persuasive secular vision: the individual is prevented from reaching her or his full humanity by the systems that control individuals. Perhaps a pungent truth *is* present in this vision: groups and the political or economic systems they create can and do crush people. Just read the first two chapters of the Book of Exodus. It's when the suggestion is made that the capacity to control or dominate others dwells within the human psyche or heart that people get jumpy, especially if one believes that reasonable people don't do or at least don't intend to do harm to others. If people are basically good or reasonable or teachable, how does one account not only for the global crises of our age but also the seemingly mundane ways in which suffering can stream through our daily experience? Ask Adam, pointing his finger at Eve: "The woman whom you gave to be with me, she gave me fruit from the tree, and I ate" (Gen. 3:12). Don't blame me; it's her fault, not mine. Or ask the German Christian soldier who shut the crematorium door in a Nazi concentration camp. "I was just following orders." I'm not going to take responsibility for my actions. And so there it is: Blame the other. Not me. It's her fault. It's his fault.

To say it as clearly as possible: Christianity does not affirm the natural perfection of humanity. Rather, it claims that God desires the full flourishing of everything God creates. It praises God as the One who gives strength to humans and all living things. But it also recognizes the presence of dehumanizing forces in the world and claims that humans actually find themselves struggling in this force field of evil, ignorance, and sickness, both suffering from it and participating in it. In this view, babies don't spring from the womb naturally good or perfect. Oh, they may be cute and precious, but they find themselves in this force field that may be gracious and loving but is also marked by suffering and just plain bad luck. An older confession articulates the dilemma in this manner:

> Most merciful God,
> We confess that we are in bondage to sin and cannot free
>   ourselves.
> We have sinned against you in thought, word, and deed,
> by what we have done and by what we have left undone.
> We have not loved you with our whole heart;
> we have not loved our neighbors as ourselves.

> For the sake of your Son, Jesus Christ, have mercy on us.
> Forgive us, renew us, and lead us.
> (*Lutheran Book of Worship*, p. 56)

Lest one imagine that this confession is the work of a committee intent on making everyone feel miserable at the beginning of the liturgy, think again. It is simply the articulation of a Christian realism rooted in the biblical vision of life and confirmed by human experience. Forces beyond human control pull apart life. The Greek word for that pulling apart is "dia-bolein," to throw apart, from whence comes the English word *diabolic*. What's "diabolical" is not a sinister man clothed in red tights with horns and tail sprouting from his body. What is diabolical is the reality of human suffering, being pulled apart, unhealthy, "unwhole." Adam and Eve are pulled apart from each other and from the God who brought them to life. The way many early Christian writers spoke of this primordial "pulling apart" was in the language of servitude or slavery, a reality of life in the ancient world. Humans cannot free themselves from the desire to be more than human. They desire to be gods. They cannot reconcile themselves to being a creature among creatures and all that entails: limited knowledge, the struggle to survive, bad luck, and mortality. While Greek philosophers would dream of perfection in another world, the Hebrew mind was focused on the gritty realities of life and human limitation. The strong—both individuals and groups— overpower the weak. The mighty—both bosses and nations—enslave the vulnerable. The clever wiggle out of the demands of justice.

Luther calls this potent reality being "curved inward." It is nothing less than a rigorous rebellion against being a creature among creatures, dependent on God and the goodness of what God offers all living things. It is the capacity to think of the lone self as the center of the universe of one's own imagining, thus absolving oneself of any responsibility for that which God offers freely and graciously to all living creatures. It is, to say the least, a deeply "psychological" view of the human person from one of the most introspective thinkers in the history of the West. Humankind is intended to serve as wise and responsible creatures in this world, but another capacity is alive as well: the capacity to overwork and erode, pollute and poison, hoard and waste the good things of the earth with impunity. No one should need a theologian or a preacher to be convinced of the disastrous consequences of this turning inward. Remember the newspaper reports?

One of the signs of imagining the self to be the "subject" who sits at the center of one's own little universe is the sense that the big "I" is not dependent on anyone or anything else in life. People become objects to serve the will. My students know something about this when I ask them if they know what it feels like to be "objectified." "You feel less than human, almost subhuman," said one psychology major, "as if you have nothing to offer the other person, as if you, oh, as if you're somehow nothing!" If I am the one valid "subject" in "my" world, then it is remarkably easy to recognize others as "objects" rather than subjects in their own right, creatures with me in this world, members of a common creation. To confess "we have not loved our neighbor as ourselves" is to claim that one does not recognize the neighbor (Eve, the Jew, the stranger, that other culture, that race or nation) as a distinctive creation of God, as another subject in the world who really doesn't need to be controlled.

Keep no score of wrong

For Christians, Jesus of Nazareth stands as the One turned fully toward God and neighbor. Indeed, is it not the command he gives that sums up the entire Law: to love God and to love one's neighbor as oneself (Mark 12:28-34)? Proclaimed the beloved one of God in his baptism, the gospels offer the good news that this one reveals what Luther called "the gracious heart of God," that is, a God who desires "life, health, and salvation" for the children of earth. Rather than being focused on the self, on the great "I" to the exclusion of others, Jesus was turned toward them. He was, as it were, *reconciled* to being a human among humans, in love with them, open to them, serving them simply because it benefited them. Does such an assertion cast Jesus as wispy do-gooder? Or, as feminist Christians have made necessarily clear, does such an assertion simply reinforce the stereotype of woman as domestic servant to active, public man? Well, it has and it could, that is unless it is placed next to the stories of Jesus giving women and many others a sense of their own God-given agency in the world. It should come as no surprise, then, that Paul interprets the mission of Jesus as one of both liberation and reconciliation: liberation from the powers that dehumanize and crush life and the reconciliation of all things into the gracious intentions of God. Yet, easier said than done. Keep in mind the news reports.

In the world of the ancient Mediterranean and the one reported in the media, another law abides. Rent any of the *Godfather* films and one sees it clearly. It is the law of retribution: You hurt me; I hurt you back. It is the simplest form of "justice," pervasive and instinctual. A one-year-old has his ball taken away from him by another toddler and proceeds to bop the thief on the head. Crying ensues and only the watchful eyes of parents who laugh at the mischief avert further toddler fighting. Played out on a regional or global scale, however, it doesn't appear so harmless. No way out of retribution appears; what some call a cycle of violence extends from one generation to the next, never fully satisfied that revenge has been sufficient or complete. Ask the Palestinians and the Israelis or any seasoned divorce lawyer. The wounds, physical and psychological, are deep in the memory of the body. People are naturally perfect? It may not be too far-fetched to argue that people can certainly be in "bondage" to retribution or revenge.

We also know of another form of justice, a step up and away from the perpetual cycle born in revenge. It is woven into the code of law that governs most people throughout the world. If someone breaks the law through theft, embezzlement, or murder, for instance, the law prescribes a compensating punishment: a fine, prison sentence, or death in some states and regions. I am not allowed to take the car of the thief who stole mine, or murder the spouse of the one who killed a relative. This form of justice may have been served, yet it brings no reconciliation between victim and perpetrator.

When the New Testament speaks of reconciliation, it is referring to something much different from revenge or appropriate punishment. It is referring to the experience of restoration or reconciliation. One might argue that it is the most difficult and the most life-giving form of justice to enact. It forgoes retribution and punishment. Instead, it actively seeks the restoration of relationship between persons or groups who are estranged, alienated from each other. It is nothing less than the power of forgiveness: the capacity to actually feel the experience of estrangement and yet release the claim to reprisal or punishment. And it is in that release from a life marked by resentment that hope appears, the frailest of shoots planted in the soil of human experience.

A most eloquent testament to the power of forgiveness in the world today is the imperfect yet unprecedented experiment launched in South Africa at the end of the brutal, demeaning, and death-dealing experience of apartheid. How would we go forward, asked Desmond Tutu, the Anglican Archbishop of Capetown. Revenge would be so easy and punishment of criminals would fill the jails. Yet would it bring any healing of the nation, any reconciliation that could give rise to hope out of a most ghastly situation? Appointed by President Mandela as the chair of South Africa's Truth and Reconciliation Commission, Archbishop Tutu supervised the establishment of this central Christian practice in its political form: the opportunity for people, estranged by discrimination and bloody violence, to face each other, speak the truth, and ask for forgiveness. Here in a lengthy and painful process, women and men who witnessed or were the objects of terrible torture and maiming were called forth to face their oppressors with the truth of what happened to them, their families, or friends. As Tutu narrates the process in *No Future Without Forgiveness*, forgiveness is not overlooking the tedious or the horrific dimensions of human alienation or estrangement. Without truth telling, how can reconciliation take hold in life? Any therapist worth his or her salt will tell you the same.

No future without forgiveness

No wonder, then, that the ecumenical pattern of worship invites the worshiping assembly to keep silence for reflection and self-examination before the gathering confesses together and then hears the announcement of forgiveness. What happens, however, if no silence is kept to create a space in which people can face the truth about themselves, their relationships, or the estrangement of the world? Does the subsequent announcement of forgiveness sound like just so many empty words addressed to a moderately attentive crowd that, perhaps, doesn't have time or the desire to face the truth? Or is it possible that most North American Christians would accept Anne Frank's dictum that human beings are basically good; people who may slip up on occasion and simply need a second chance? If we don't really do much harm to each other or stand passively in its presence, then who needs silence?

It makes one wonder, then, why the Christian liturgy is suffused with words and gestures devoted to reconciliation, as if the liturgy were a boot camp for people who live in a world that needs both truth and reconciliation:

> God of all mercy and consolation, come the aid of your people
> Christ, have mercy
> The peace of Christ be with you
> Forgive us our sins as we forgive those who sin against us

> Lamb of God, you take away the sin of the world
> For you and all people for the forgiveness of sin
> You have refreshed us through the healing power of this gift of life
> (RW6, pp. 6, 8, 9, 12, 14, 15, 17)

If you think about it long enough, one could imagine that the entire Christian liturgy, from beginning to end, is nothing less than one grand offer, one enactment in word and gesture, one compelling call to receive and tenaciously grasp what Paul calls the ministry of reconciliation (2 Cor. 5:18). That, of course, presumes that one has the courage to recognize the truth and the desire to promote reconciliation in a world marked by far too much suffering. Is it not ironic that in the same century when human beings created the means to destroy the earth in a nuclear conflagration that the words and gesture of Peace were restored to the liturgy? Is there any reason more compelling to practice, week in and week out, the gestures of reconciling peace at the moment when humans could face the dreaded consequences of "irreconcilable differences" between the nations of the earth? Although many people on a Sunday morning might think that the exchange of Peace is simply a time to say Hello to one's neighbor, the biblical inspiration for the placement of the gesture before coming to the table is worth noting. In the context of the Sermon on the Mount, the Matthean Jesus says:

> When you are offering your gift at the altar,
> if you remember that your brother or sister has something
>   against you,
> leave your gift there before the altar and go;
> first be reconciled to your brother or sister,
> and then come and offer your gift.
> (Matt. 5:23-24)

A former professor once said to me, "The Peace is the happiest three minutes in the liturgy when you get to greet everyone around you." Maybe so, maybe so. Yet at one African American parish in the Midwest, the "passing of the peace" usually takes twenty minutes. "We take those words about reconciling seriously," said the pastor. "With all the shootings and beatings in our neighborhood, we never know for sure if we're going to see each other come next Sunday. We want to eat and drink and then leave at peace with each other."

Toward the end of the Gospel of John, we find the disciples locked up in a house, terrified, fearful of what awaits them outside. It is not a friendly neighborhood. The disciples are also fully aware that they abandoned—even betrayed—Jesus. To say the least, a whole lot of psychic pain is reverberating throughout the place. That is, until the risen Christ appears to them and simply says, "Peace be with you." He shows them his wounds—he lets them see the truth of his suffering—but offers no blame, no castigation. And then the most surprising thing happens: he breathes into them the ministry of forgiveness that is to be extended to the ends of the earth (John 20:19-23). The peace, the wounds, the sending. Is it a coincidence that the liturgy follows the biblical pattern in word and gesture: the greeting of peace, the showing and offering of the wounds in bread and cup, and the dismissal?

"God so loved the world that he gave his only Son," says the Johannine Christ (John 3:16). As a young boy I believed that God's forgiveness was given to me and me alone, a child who frequently broke the rules of home, church, and school. My, what an understandable but impoverished view! Even though one may imagine that God's love manifested as forgiveness is only for me, the word John uses is *cosmos*, the world. The forgiveness that one receives through communion in the wounds of Christ is intended to grasp one for the work of forgiveness and reconciliation *in the world*. Yet to enter such a world and promote reconciliation may lead one into trouble, into the world reported in the news. It is so much easier to stay locked up in the house, fearful of that world. It is so much easier, when estranged, hurt, or crushed, to follow the path of resentment and revenge. Maybe nice people, good people don't need this gift. Yet that pesky archbishop from South Africa keeps saying, again and again, the world has *no future without forgiveness.* One wonders: will the gift ever be unleashed beyond the doors of the church's house?

For reflection and discussion

1. What are the sources that have shaped your view of humanity? What do these sources lead you to conclude about the human condition?

2. Many of the eighteenth-century founding figures in the United States believed that all people were good and endowed with reason. Such a view has led political figures to emphasize the optimism of the American spirit. Consequently, Luther's view of humanity "turned inward" does not find a welcome home in much of America. What do you think is the value in Luther's view for the larger culture?

3. The Christian liturgy invites people to tell the truth about their "sin," their being turned away from God and the neighbor in need. What would you consider the value in keeping such a confession on a regular if not weekly basis in your life or your congregation's life?

4. A sense of restorative justice welcomes forgiveness as the means through which relationship with others is restored. Have you ever experienced restoration of relationship in the context of Christian worship? If so, what prompted this healing of relationship?

5. In the liturgy, Christians sing, "Lamb of God, you take away the sin of the world: have mercy on us." The text, from John's gospel, focuses on the world. As a freely forgiven people, how might Christians serve this world, frequently torn by racial, economic, and political strife, through the promotion of reconciliation?

6
To Give Ourselves Away As Bread for the Hungry

The world in which Christians break bread

At the turn of the last century, my paternal grandfather, Silas Benjamin Torvend, moved from California to the Pacific Northwest. Arriving by horse-drawn wagon, he settled on farmland near Silverton, Oregon, in the verdant Willamette Valley. For many years, he and my grandmother, Emma Pedersen, lived in a home warmed by a wood-burning stove and lighted by kerosene lamps. Their connection to the larger world was through hand-delivered mail and one local newspaper.

In the year my grandparents moved to Oregon, the United States entered the First World War. Within a year, they were reading in the Oregon papers that "modern warfare" had been forever changed, with devastating results, by the invention and use of mustard gas and the moving tank. Yet, despite the Great War and the Great Depression, they, along with countless farming families, were creating in the western reaches of this nation one of the largest agricultural centers in the world. Their enthusiasm for farming was supported by America's seemingly unbounded hope in the future, a hope rooted in the technological application of western scientific advances. Indeed, the couple who arrived at their future farm on a horse-drawn wagon would eventually fly in Boeing jets across the country and watch an American walk on the moon's surface with a golf club in hand.

By the time of their deaths, they had witnessed the shift from a society rooted in the slower movement of farm and factory to one shaped and dominated by the ever-accelerating pace of digital communication and a global market economy poised to run continuously around the clock, each and every day of the year. I am old enough to remember when a postcard from my grandparents took five days to reach our home in California. Were they alive today, I could send them an e-mail in five seconds.

At the time of their retirement, lobbing mustard gas into a trench and rolling tanks through the French countryside seemed like child's play compared to the "efficiency" of dropping a single nuclear bomb on a city or lacing its watershed with a drop of toxic poison. As North Americans may only vaguely recognize, the most dramatic challenges to the optimistic dream of the Enlightenment, a dream that fueled the imagination of western Europeans and North Americans for three hundred years, took place in the middle of the last century when six million Jews and six million gypsies, homosexuals, political prisoners, and disabled persons were exterminated in and around a country that claimed to be the world leader in advanced scientific research and educational excellence. I know that my parents and grandparents rejoiced with millions of people throughout the world at end of the Second World War, an end brought about by the bright flash of atomic light. Perhaps it was only later that some of them understood with utter clarity the significance of the dropping of two small bombs over Japan.

My grandparents were among the many Americans who rejoiced at the pleasure of driving on the extensive road system that was in place by the late 1950s. Yet when they moved to Los Angeles twenty years later, they could see the heavy pollution filling the air they were breathing. Although they probably never heard the terms *global warming* or *environmental degradation*, they witnessed their effects on a daily basis.

These examples are not intended to demonize scientific advancement and technological expertise. Human curiosity, inventiveness, and hard work brought us air conditioning, antibiotics, and increased grain yields. Such labor also produced smart bombs, biological warfare, and famine. The examples simply show how, in the past hundred years, much of the world has experienced a shift in perception unprecedented in human history.

First, we know that human beings hold in their hands the means to destroy human life on this planet in unimaginable numbers. We may be genuinely grateful that we can e-mail our friends and write reports or books on computers, but we know that with five to ten clicks of the mouse, it's possible to access a plan for a low-grade chemical weapon. No one in the history the world could have imagined that with five or six bombs, entire regions of the world could experience a nuclear winter that would snuff the life out of land, air, and water.

Second, we know what no previous generation could have thought possible, that the survival of the planet and all its life forms would become an open question. While considerable debate rages over the long-term effects of global warming, considerable agreement is also heard concerning the failure of some First World nations to join others in an intentional and coordinated project to ensure the survival and flourishing of bodies of water, diverse species, clean air, and renewable land use. Does this sound alarmist? Maybe. It's just that no one here will swim and fish in the major rivers that were, less than a hundred years ago, fresh and crystal clear. Will the planet survive human domination and oppression? The jury is still out.

Third, North Americans are among the wealthiest people on the face of the earth. We boast one of the highest concentrations of top medical research centers in the world. We consider ourselves a deeply charitable people. Yet, at the same time, the most recent governmental reports, confirmed by independent research institutes, indicate soaring levels of child malnourishment throughout the land. North Americans may consider themselves members of the First World, yet 14 percent of the same population lives in Third World conditions. Who knew? Physical violence, sexual misconduct, financial crimes, and political scandal are attention-grabbing headlines. Kids going hungry every day is news that just doesn't have quite the same "zip" as a movie star's overdose. From my office I look out on a neatly manicured campus where one can find an assortment of cafeterias and restaurants. Yet within blocks of the university, hundreds of children live without adequate food and drink.

Some would say we live in a postmodern age. Perhaps.

I would suggest this: we live in a time never before imagined in the history of the world.

Consolation and entertainment

Here is the argument: The critical situation we face today, a situation larger than the churches, actually influences the lives of people who search for a church community or regularly participate in its worship. It is a situation in which the rapid rate of change in technical advances, the current movement to a global economy, and increasing demand for options in our cultural life are compounded by environmental and military threats. To say the least, such a situation creates a sense of anxiety and helplessness. "What can one person do to protect the planet?" my students plead. And when people are anxious or helpless, when they feel threatened, they can become preoccupied with themselves. It is an understandable and natural instinct.

Maybe many people, in fact, *are* aware of this new situation in which we find ourselves, a situation utterly unimaginable to our immigrant forebearers. We don't really know whether the planet will survive pollution and degradation, and yet we show up for work, catch a ball game, pay bills, celebrate birthdays, make love, watch the evening news, and take vacations. Maybe people do all these things because they are simply optimistic or possessed of a profound hope rooted in faith. We don't know whether anyone can protect us from terrorist attacks or whether Korea will experience armed conflict that could spill across the Pacific. But my guess is that many of us don't think about it that much. And so I make out course schedules, mow the lawn, pay my taxes, and go to movies.

Or we may be vaguely aware that almost every revolution and mass movement of the nineteenth and twentieth centuries—whether the Bolshevik uprising or the continual stream of laborers across this nation's southern border—can be discerned as the search by hungry people for bread, for nourishment, for life. My guess is that most people reading these words are well fed and educated, two common realities that can, nonetheless, blind us to the growing hunger epidemic across the land. So we may be deeply charitable toward the needy and yet recognize that we may never find ourselves among those who have no bread and no cup, an awkward position that places us firmly within the pragmatic "wisdom" of our age: The strong survive; the weak perish.

Yet I would argue that this new situation is *not* something that theologians, educators, musicians, pastors, artists, bishops, or lay people ought to overlook. Oh, we may readily be aware of the larger threats to the earth and its people, but in order to survive, in order to make the most of life now, we may place such thoughts on the shelf of the unconscious and close the cupboard door. Or we may simply imagine that other people—scientists, the military, diplomats, or humanitarian groups—will serve as the buffer between our lives and the larger forces that can undo an "American way of life."

Edward Farley, Emeritus Professor of Theology at Vanderbilt University, writes that "individuals [in church] communities spend

most of their time and energy in nonchurch environments." He
continues:

> As [individuals in church communities] pass from childhood to
> adulthood and as they pursue leisure activities, work in busi-
> nesses, and exist in families and other [small groups], they
> imbibe the anxieties, narcissism, and individualism [of this cul-
> ture]." Consequently, "church communities are filled with anx-
> ious individuals . . . dominated by the need for consolation,
> distraction, reassurance, and entertainment" (*Deep Symbols*, pp.
> 67–68).

Such a sense of anxiety or narcissism is not necessarily debilitating,
that is *if* one lives in a culture that values strong family or friendship
ties, ensures the means of survival for all its citizens, and places great
emphasis on the common good. In this kind of atmosphere, people
can recognize that they are not alone, strengthen each other through
the bonds of friendship, and cultivate an ethic of care for each other
and the earth. The difficulty for North Americans is that the dominant cultural images or messages tell us it is a person's duty to go it
alone, to leave one's family and never return, to compete aggressively
with colleagues or global neighbors. North Americans are expected to
be mobile and rootless because it is how corporate life in a global
market economy is conducted. Believe me, I don't have a single student who imagines that he or she will hold the same job for a lifetime
or live in the same place for more than five years. The future is open
to rootless wanderers. Consequently, in this cultural context, a sense
of anxiety, helplessness, or self-preoccupation can be readily rein-
forced by the common expectation that people are to "make it" on
their own.

How does this reality play out in the life of a congregation? Is it
possible that many people *unconsciously* expect that a congregation
and its worship offer (1) a sense of comfort or peace of mind for

people who feel anxious and (2) distracting entertainments to those who are fearful in a threatened world? One need only consider again the work of Robert Bellah who examined the narrowing of the American religious imagination to the self and a sense of personal well-being, to recognize that over and frequently against the communal and prophetic language of the Bible and Christian worship, many who participate in Christian communities expect and even demand that such worship communicate a sense of personal comfort or powerful inspiration.

Breathing in and breathing out

In such a context and with such expectations, the movement of Christian worship can begin to look deeply *centripetal*: that is, people seek a "peaceful" center; they are drawn inward, away from a periphery that may appear threatening. Such a movement should come as no surprise. After all, if one can speak metaphorically of the assembly as a "body," it follows that a body, a worshiping body, must *breathe in* air, *drink* water, and *ingest* food in order to survive. Rightfully, one might say that people are drawn into the center of Christian worship and its supper. To participate in a community of word, baptism, and supper is to be gathered into the community of the Holy Three and this local community gathered around Bible, font, and table. Thus, the centripetal movement of the liturgy—the assembly being gathered in the name and presence of the diverse community of the Trinity—can, indeed, readily respond to the aching need alive in our anxious time for a meaningful center where a merciful and consoling "word" may be proclaim and received.

Yet one of the core insights of Luther and the reforming movement that bears his name is the insistence that the Lord's supper enacts God's movement in Christ *toward and beyond* the worshiping assembly. The supper announces, as it were, *Jesus Christ given for the life of the world* in word and sign.

> When you have partaken of this sacrament [the Lord's Supper],
> you must in turn share the misfortunes of the fellowship. . . .
> Here your heart must go out in love and learn that this is a
> sacrament of love. As love and support are given you, you in
> turn must render love and support to Christ in his needy ones.
> You must feel with sorrow all the unjust suffering of the inno-
> cent, with which the world is everywhere filled to overflowing.
> You must fight, work, pray, and—if you cannot do more—have
> heartfelt sympathy. [For] here the saying of Paul is fulfilled,
> "Bear one another's burdens, and so fulfill the law of Christ"
> [Gal. 6:2] (*Luther's Works,* vol. 35, p. 54).

With this admonition, Luther clearly announces the *centrifugal* movement of the Word of God, of the liturgy, and the Christian assembly. With breathing in, the body must also breathe out in order to survive. Set next to the centripetal movement of gathering inward is the centrifugal movement of sending outward into a beautiful and threatening world. Perhaps, then, the expectation is too small that a pastor will simply speak God's love "for me"—the little self. Too small may be the expectation that Christian worship needs to communicate a feeling of peace for the individual or one's family or my like-mind-ed friends in one's comfortable but threatened social location. Indeed, the centrifugal movement of the liturgy can be readily thwarted by the expectation that here, at last, the people will find a refuge from that threatening world filled with weapons or terrorists or frighten-ing homeless people who beg for bread on public streets.

In contrast, the function of the gospel, communicated through the word preached and the word enacted in the supper, is to free people from self-preoccupation, from anxiety and helplessness. Its purpose is to comfort the assembly, that is, *to give strength* in the presence of threatening foes. But to fulfill this purpose, the truth about our life and the larger world that shapes our lives must be heard in the assem-bly. To imagine that the Christian community and its worship is a flight from this real world and its deadly serious problems, and to accede to the demand for a world-escaping entertainment would be to compromise the very heart of the gospel: *God is with humanity in this world.* God is not a refuge from the world; God is refuge *in* the world. The preposition makes all the difference: not "from" but "in." Is it any wonder, then, that the supper concludes with words of service? "By your Spirit strengthen us to serve all in want and give ourselves away as bread for the hungry. . . . Go in peace. Serve the Lord" (RW6, pp. 17–18).

Instructions for sharing bread

In the culture where we break bread, many people tend to see religion as a source of comfort or an inspirational break from "life in the world." The expectation is also alive that the Christ proclaimed by the liturgy will simply conform to culturally formed expectations or values. Yet the gospels offer us another perspective. New Testament scholar Marianne Sawicki writes:

> The epistles and the gospels were written to convey memories about Jesus from those who had known him before [his death] to those who wanted to know him afterward. But in addition to *memories,* these texts were written to convey *instructions* for recognizing the Lord in real time, that is, for finding Jesus incognito in our present circumstances. [Of course] memories are easier to accept than instructions, because memories refer back to a past time; what they recall is presumed to be settled and closed. Thus it is relatively easy for us . . . to take up bread and cup *in remembrance* of the fact that Jesus lived here once upon a time. It is much less [easy] to seek Jesus in the present, even though we know where he is dwelling. It is difficult to worship *in expectation* of . . . responding to the invitations he gives us right now in the needs of the hungry, the thirsty, and the homeless (Matt. 25:31-40). Their pleas for help are coming from Jesus incognito ("What is 'contemporary' worship?" p. 29).

What might this mean, then, for those who break bread now in a world filled with hungry people? Between a gathering and a sending forth in the liturgy, do Christians not receive broken bread—a broken body—in order to learn to recognize the Risen One present in broken and hungry bodies? Is not one gift of this thanksgiving meal, this Lord's supper, this Holy Communion, the instruction to go forth, to be sent outward? No wonder the ancient Latin word for dismissal, *missa*, became the "Mass," the most frequently used word for Christian worship in the West, as if the entire liturgy were focused on sending into the world rather than trying to escape it. "The Mass is retained among us and is celebrated with the greatest reverence," notes the Augsburg Confession (*The Book of Concord*, p. 69). The "sending outward" is retained among us, one might say.

But sending outward to what end? Even though conservative evangelicals are eager to transform the world into one large Sunday school and the more radical wings of the Protestant reformation suggest the church survive as an alternative culture to contemporary secular culture, Luther's ecumenical vision holds another promise and challenge: When you have partaken of this sacrament, you must fight, work, pray in a world filled with suffering. It would seem that "conquering for Christ" or protesting from a holy enclave is rejected. Rather, the baptismal and eucharistic vocation leads one to engage this world in costly service. Is it any wonder that the One who refused to count equality with God something to be grasped at, emptied himself into the form of a servant (Phil. 2:6-7)? Is it any wonder that a theology of the cross would lead one to become attentive to real suffering in the world? Is it any wonder that such a steady gaze on this suffering would move one with compassion to share bread with those who are hungry and on the margins? Is it any wonder that in the midst of breaking bread in the world one might just ask the troubling question: Why is such charity necessary in a world of plenty? If any truth is found in Sawicki's claim, then it would seem that the gift of the holy meal is more a question: Where is Christ hidden in the suffering of the world, calling the assembly to his sisters and brothers? What are the central things of Christian worship? A participating assembly, a book of promises carefully proclaimed and interpreted for the assembly's life in the world, an open welcome to the needs and suffering of the larger world in prayer, a font or pool where the words and water of life consecrate each one to public service in the world, a meal of real bread and wine offered indiscriminately to all hungry people, and this, too: a sending into the world. At the conclusion of his gospel, Luke narrates an encounter that sets forth what would become the pattern of Christian worship:

> A stranger comes to disciples on the road.
> Together the three form a little community.
> The risen Christ interprets all the things written about him in
>   the scriptures.
> They gather at table where he takes the bread of the earth.
> He gives thanks to God, breaks it apart, and gives it to them
> They recognize who he is in the breaking of the bread.

Here is the remarkable end of the story or its very beginning: they do not return quietly to their homes or escape to the hills. Rather, they get up and *enter the city*, a place of seeming failure and grief, that Lucan metaphor of the larger world, and share good news with a group of people experiencing nothing less than collective paralysis. They come with neither apathy nor fear but with the gospel they received in word and sign. They have been graciously freed from despair and enabled to serve in the world.

So, then, this gift, too: broken and poured at table to be broken and poured out into the world.

> God has charged us:
> and how can we but ask
> for wisdom for the Christly task?

God has charged us:
and let us labor with our lives.
("God Has Called Us," *O Blessed Spring*, p. 23)

For reflection and discussion

1. What expectations do you have of the worship in your congregation? Are they largely personal (focused on you and/or your family), communal (focused on the people in the congregation), or social (focused on life in the larger world)?

2. In what ways do you sense the concerns and crises of the larger world are heard in your congregation's celebration of the eucharist?

3. Sawicki writes that the gospels offer instructions to contemporary Christians as to where they will find Jesus "incognito." Does her claim ring true or false in your experience of the Christian worship? If true, describe how it has happened.

4. If you can, relate an experience of the eucharist that challenged you to think about your engagement as a Christian in a social crisis or issue.

5. In your experience, how has the liturgy of Holy Communion moved you toward service in the world?

Ollie Mae Mills Kjesbu's Molasses Raisin Bread

1. Scald 2 cups of milk. Pour milk into a large mixing bowl.
2. Dissolve 4–5 dry packages of yeast into ¼–½ cup of lukewarm water and add 1 teaspoon sugar.
3. Melt ½ cup of shortening and mix into milk. When yeast has dissolved and become foamy, add it to the milk.
4. Add ⅓ cup sugar and ½ cup (a *full* ½ cup) of molasses. Then add 1 tablespoon of salt.
5. Gently mix all of the above ingredients. Then slowly add 6–7 cups of flour (*not* the quick-rising kind).
6. In the meantime, soak 1 cup of golden raisins for an hour or so in at least 1 cup of slightly warmed brandy. If no brandy is available, soak the raisins in warm water until soft. Squeeze out all the moisture before adding the raisins to the dough.
7. Add the cup of raisins to the dough. Knead on a floured board. (You will know that you have added enough flour if, after kneading in the flour, you can hold the palm of your hand on the dough, count to 60, and lift your hand without it sticking to the dough.)
8. Let rise until double in bulk. Shape into loaves (about 3) and let rise until double in bulk again.
9. Bake in lightly greased or buttered glass dishes or on a greased baking sheet at 350 degrees for 45–60 minutes.
10. Brush melted butter over freshly baked bread after taking from the oven.

—*As written in her own hand by Alice Kjesbu Torvend*

Bibliography

Foundational Texts

Holy Communion and Related Rites. Renewing Worship, vol. 6. Minneapolis: Augsburg Fortress, 2004. (All textual references to this resource are indicated by the abbreviation "RW6.")

Kolb, Robert, and Timothy J. Wengert, eds. *The Book of Concord.* Minneapolis: Fortress Press, 2000.

Luther, Martin. *Luther's Works,* vol. 35. Ed. Theodore Bachman and trans. Jeremiah Schindel. Philadelphia: Muhlenberg Press, 1960.

Lutheran Book of Worship. Minneapolis: Augsburg Publishing House and Philadelphia: Board of Publication, Lutheran Church in America, 1978.

With One Voice: A Lutheran Resource for Worship. Minneapolis: Augsburg Fortress, 1995.

Introduction

Lathrop, Gordon. *What are the essentials of Christian worship?* Open Questions in Worship, vol. 1. Minneapolis: Augsburg Fortress, 1994.

Tillich, Paul. "Symbols of Faith" in *Dynamics of Faith.* New York: Harper , 1957.

1. Let the Vineyards Be Fruitful

Lathrop, Gordon. "Eucharist and Earth-Care," *Holy Ground: A Liturgical Cosmology*. Minneapolis: Fortress Press, 2003.

Santmire, H. Paul. *Nature Reborn: The Ecological and Cosmic Promise of Christian Theology*. Minneapolis: Fortress Press, 2000.

2. To Give Our Thanks and Praise

Browning, Elizabeth Barrett. "Aurora Leigh. A Poem." London: J. Miller, 1864. Online at http://digital.library.upenn.edu/women/barrett/aurora/aurora.html.

Jenks, Alan. "Eating and Drinking in the Old Testament," *Anchor Bible Dictionary* 2. New York: Doubleday, 1992.

Ramshaw, Gail. "Food," *Treasures Old and New: Images in the Lectionary*. Minneapolis, Fortress Press, 2002.

3. Breaking Bread with the Outcast

Hanson, K. C., and Douglas Oakman. *Palestine in the Time of Jesus: Social Structures and Social Conflicts*. Minneapolis: Fortress Press, 1998.

Smith, Dennis. *From Symposium to Eucharist: The Banquet in the Early Christian World*. Minneapolis: Fortress Press, 2003.

Snyder, Graydon. "Food and Meals," *Inculturation of the Jesus Tradition: The Impact of Jesus on Jewish and Roman Cultures*. Harrisburg, PA: Trinity Press International, 1999.

4. Pour Us Out for Each Other

Baptism, Eucharist and Ministry. Faith and Order Paper No. 111. Geneva: World Council of Churches, 1982.

Bellah, Robert. *Habits of the Heart: Individualism and Commitment in American Life*. Berkeley: University of California Press, 1985.

Lathrop, Gordon. *Holy People: A Liturgical Ecclesiology*. Minneapolis: Fortress Press, 1999.

Minear, Paul. *Images of the Church in the New Testament*. Philadelphia: Westminster Press, 1960.

Stauffer, S. Anita, ed. *Worship and Culture in Dialogue*. Geneva: Lutheran World Federation, 1994.

5. Have Mercy on Us

Bonhoeffer, Dietrich. *The Cost of Discipleship*. New York: Macmillan, 1963.

Henderson, Frank. *Liturgy, Justice, and the Reign of God: Integrating Vision and Practice*. http://www.compusmart.ab.ca/fhenders/pdf/LJRG.pdf.

Moe-Lobeda, Cynthia. *Healing a Broken World: Globalization and God*. Minneapolis: Augsburg Fortress, 2002.

Tutu, Desmond. *No Future Without Forgiveness*. New York: Doubleday, 1999

6. To Give Ourselves Away As Bread for the Hungry

Bushkofsky, Dennis *Share Your Bread: World Hunger and Worship*. Chicago: ELCA, 2000.

Cherwien, Susan Palo. *O Blessed Spring*. Minneapolis: Augsburg Fortress, 1997.

Farley, Edward. *Deep Symbols: Their Postmodern Effacement and Reclamation*. Valley Forge, PA: Trinity International, 1996.

Lathrop, Gordon, ed. *What are the ethical implications of worship?* Open Questions in Worship, vol. 6. Minneapolis: Augsburg Fortress, 1996.

———. *What is contemporary worship?* Open Questions in Worship, vol. 2. Minneapolis: Augsburg Fortress, 1995.

Ramshaw, Gail. "The Poor," *Treasures Old and New: Images in the Lectionary*. Minneapolis: Fortress Press, 2002.

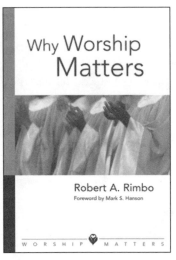

Why Worship Matters
by Robert A. Rimbo
Foreword by
Mark S. Hanson

Why Worship Matters is the first volume in a series that is an outgrowth of the Renewing Worship project of the Evangelical Lutheran Church in America. This little volume is a conversation-starter for those who want to look at the assembly's worship in very broad terms. It also invites reflection on the needs of the world, individuals, the church, and society in light of the assembly's central activity, worshiping God.

08066-5108-3

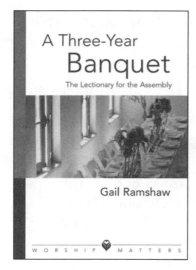

A Three-Year Banquet: The Lectionary for the Assembly

by Gail Ramshaw

A Three-Year Banquet invites the entire worshiping assembly, lay and clergy, to understand and delight in the three-year lectionary. The study guide explains how the Revised Common Lectionary was developed and how the gospels, the first readings, and the epistles are assigned. Further chapters describe many ways that the three readings affect the assembly's worship and the assembly itself. Like food at a banquet, the fare we enjoy in the lectionary nourishes us year after year.

0-8066-5105-9

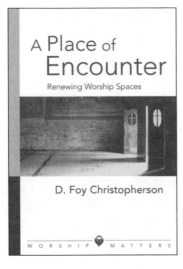

A Place of Encounter: Renewing Worship Spaces

by D. Foy Christopherson

House, temple, theatre, warehouse, courtroom, auditorium, TV studio, or lecture hall? River or baptistery or pool? Dining room or catacomb? House of God or house of the church? In its 2000-year history the church has tried on many buildings, and is ever seeking a more comfortable skin. Exactly what that skin will look like is guided by how the church understands itself, by how it worships, and by what it understands its mission to be. *A Place of Encounter* brings clarity and insight to congregations and individuals who are interested in exploring how our worship spaces serve, form, and proclaim.

0-8066-5107-5